AF334373

FIVE
on the
WESTERN EDGE

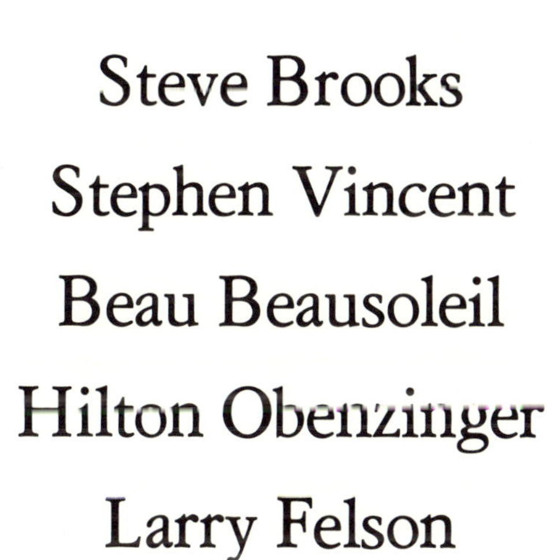

Steve Brooks

Stephen Vincent

Beau Beausoleil

Hilton Obenzinger

Larry Felson

MOMO'S PRESS   1977   SAN FRANCISCO

Cover illustration by Michael Myers.
Color production by George Mattingly.
Design and composition by Graham Mackintosh in Santa Barbara.

Poems in this work have occurred in some of the following magazines: Beatitude, Bed, Bottomfish, Dacotah Territory, FITS Broadsides, Gallimaufry, Hanging Loose, Invisible City, Isthmus, Panjandrum, San Francisco Gallery, Shocks, Strange Faeces, The Foothill Quarterly, and West Coast Poetry Review.

ISBN 0-917672-00-3 (paper)   0-917672-01-1 (cloth)

This book was partially funded by a grant from the National Endowment for the Arts.

Momo's Press, P.O. Box 14061, San Francisco CA 94114

TABLE OF CONTENTS

Harness of Bone Beau Beausoleil

Moving Day   Hilton Obenzinger

Introduction

FIVE ON THE WESTERN EDGE began more than two years ago. I had the notion that by drawing four other poets together, each of us living in San Francisco, that we could make a book that would reflect the many and various obsessions of our lives. I felt that each of us had something intense and personal to say. Each of us was in our early thirties. We had each been strongly shaped by the history of the sixties and early seventies. And in a very particular sense, our work, as various as it is, was often born and certainly deeply influenced by the intense political and aesthetic battles that can shape a writer's life in this City and on this Coast.

We met regularly for over a year to bring this collection together. Some friends, who have read this book in manuscript form, wonder how the five of us could ever be in the same room at the same time. Actually most of our meetings were warm, and, at their best, broke into real discussion of the worlds out of which we came, and the daily worlds of our obsessions. There were arguments about the poems. Why did Beau never let natural, daily occurrences into his work? Why the surreal circumference, when his actual life was full of human encounter. And Hilton, wasn't he too full of the daily world, or too busy putting the personality of his politics into his poems? And wasn't Brooks too much lost in pseudo-country style midwestern speech, or wasn't his surrealism, when he was into it, terribly artful? And wasn't Larry too unimpeachable in what he thought and felt? And wasn't I too obsessively personal and psychological? And these questions would lead into discussions of our relations with our families, our mothers and fathers, and with women. But we always stopped at a certain point, as if there was an unwillingness to take it further as a group and see what would occur in our work. It was as if the first step, as is probably true to any group, had to be a pure laying of cards on the table.

What I think we have here is a truly diverse picture of who
we are. As a poet in the book, like a swimmer who tries to
describe how he or she swims, it's difficult to say much more.
Our oppositions are probably just as important as our unities. I
hope you bounce off all five of us and come out in a new place
totally your own.

Stephen Vincent

1

The Ocean in a Bottle
Steve Brooks

The Ocean in a Bottle

I don't see through you
like I said I did.
My obsession is not insight.

I am a body turned to gas
under its own pressure.

Sometimes I am lost outside my bones
and I look so hard for them

I think I see other people's bones
under their flesh.

When I feel their bones
and their flesh,
temporarily I quit looking
for my own.

I thought I found my bones
under your flesh.

When I told you
I was embarrassed to know you so well
as to become you
I was confessing a terrible emptiness.

When I look down
and see my cloudy transparency
I become afraid.

My ambition to be full
doesn't diminish you,
but makes you unbearably desirable.

I cannot become you.
I cannot fill myself with you.
If I alone ghost the space between us
I will succeed only in vacating myself.

In a Motel with Priorities

It's 12:30 AM in Elko, Nevada

I switch on the brand new cable Hitachi TV
Jack is putting his paper barnyard together

Water is dripping in the slow draining sink
There are dead bugs in the translucent light fixture

There is a small circle smashed into the wall
by the door knob

The chair doesn't fit under the desk
the heater has no manual valve

There are patches of unmatched rug
covering the worn spots on the carpet

There are no hangers in the closet

Plastic cups are wrapped
in sanitary plastic wrap

I am lying on a pink chenille bedspread
over an army blanket and starched white sheets

The bed has a metal frame
painted to look like high gloss mahogany

Jack almost has the whole thing assembled already

When we pulled in to the Western Corral Motel
at midnight

I demanded to pay under ten dollars
my limit

The man said ''$8.40''
he was ready for bed

A half-hour later
after touring the town
looking for better

I rang the bell on his pre-fab motel office
waking him up

Short fellow
He knew I wouldn't find any better

He charged me $8.50
and gave me all silver
50c and a silver dollar

I brought Julie's banana bread in with us
didn't eat any

Drank two glasses of wine
still warm from a full day of sun

I know the car won't start in the morning

I drove for three hours
knowing that if I stopped
and somehow shut off the engine

I'd never get going again

Something wrong with it

I had visions of telling Jack
how to pop the clutch

On a long grade in the middle of Nevada
in the dark

Then watching
as he drove off in the night

Alternating between desperation and complacency

''This is God's country
We are safe out here.''

''This is the forbidding surface
of a cold, cruel and uncompromising planet.''

I finally eat some banana nut bread
and drink a third glass of wine

Or is it a third plastic of wine?

Jack finishes the barnyard
and shows me a picture of Bugs Bunny

Sneaking off with the carrots
right under Elmer Fudd's nose

Earlier today I was overcharged
for a Polish strudel with gravy

And
$8.50 is an exorbitant price to pay
to keep this anachronistic
floating America alive.

At Home in Moline

As Don Juan would do to his front porch,
I wander around in my parent's house looking
for the magic spot
from which to experience everything.

Jack and Rachel get out baby toys and play with them.
I read with fascination my college yearbook.

I put on my brother's shoes,
6'2'', and he wears higher heels than I do,
shoes thin in the leather
and tight like José Greco.

There's my ex-wife's former boyfriend in a
leather jacket holding a rifle.
There's Vince Anku from Ghana standing naked
in a bath towel holding a sign, Bombs Away.
There I am holding a plastic water faucet
up to my left temple with just a trace of concern
on my face as to what's going to come pouring out.

Smoking cigarettes, drinking Cutty Sark, sitting
in my father's naugahyde lounge chair with the
stick-shift position adjuster.

I say to the kids, Here's
a picture of your mother;
can you tell which one she is?
Yeah, that's her, all right.

Here's your mom singing with Sam Schuman,
and here's me dancing.
Is that my mom?
No, that's Betsy, a girl
I used to know.

Betsy says to me, How does Julie feel
about you going out with me?
Betsy, how do you feel,
married to an ex-Cuban, two
kids later, are you wandering around
your kitchen coop reading tarot cards,
talking to ghosts like I am?

I went to the Quad-City Open today
and saw Slammin' Sammy Snead sink an
eight foot putt to tie for the lead
on the third day, 95 degrees,
drinking Hamm's Beer, talking to
my brother, telling him, Mark,
you are the only person I know who
gives me an indiscriminate running commentary
on his every inconsequential prejudice.

Women, he says, if you look at them, are
disgusted, they think every man is a lecher.

There's Wayne Gano in his underwear and
there's Jack Chapman looking like an ingenue,
a man I loved, I thought he jilted me.

Jack says, in the dark, sleeping in Cantwell's room,
a year after graduation,
You know, there's something I've wanted to say.
What, I say, You can say it, you've missed me,
right?
Uh, yeah, he says, and a slab of recognition falls on me.
He wasn't going to say that at all.
I like pizza, or President Johnson is no good,
or College was a bore, but not
I love you.

So I call up Paul tonight in California,
to hear what it sounds like to be a voice,
and who answers the phone, but my old friend Chuck.

Chuck, you asshole, I hope to God you're sleeping
in my bed.
Yeah, I sort of am, he says.

I walk by my father, and I touch him,
I caress him.

Jack cries, Rachel gets everything.
Not tonight, my son.
Tonight I love you best.

There Was a Goddess of Poetry

There was a goddess of poetry
living on our block for a week,
and tonight I went up to Paul,
and I said, You know,
it's a shame we don't go see her,
while she's here,
and he said, No, man, she's gone.

I saw a face in a window,
and I thought it was her,
clouded by curtains and cigarette smoke,
but Paul says she's gone anyway.

I could see her kitchen clearly,
refrigerator and overhead light
on the second floor.
Paul suggested I read a book.

I called a mortal woman on the phone,
and left my number to be called
for dancing later on,
if she wanted.

No Eurydice she,
I'll have to survive on my own.

After all, the goddess is gone.
No use exaggerating
what I'm left with.

The Cow Pond

My heart is beating faster.
I am at a loss trying to remember it all.
I remember the house almost exploding.
Running under the house to shut off the gas.
No curtain for the toilet.

The road winding beside a creek up to the house.
The undergrowth thick and green beside the road.
Insects. Noises at night.
Shutting the door against the dogs and the pups.
Shutting the gates after going through in cars or on horseback.
Listening to the breathing as we slept, nearly touching,
in one room.

All of us forming a caravan from Alan's house,
over the hill, to the cow pond, and swimming naked,
two miles from the ocean.

Nancy's small breasts exposed. Patricia's hidden.
Katie. I can't remember. Was she naked?
My erection growing and calmed.

Walking the horse back and forth down the steep slope,
slipping in my leather-soled shoes.

Did the police come, or the owner, or only a fisherman?

The children drowning each other.
Lying on the cracked, caked mud bank, under the rickety tower.
Was it a pumping station, or a dock when the water was higher.

The cows came but moved off when Alan yelled.
What did he yell?
And he was naked. 40 years old, a school-teacher,
asking questions.
At home, alone on the weekend,
Suddenly with visitors.

Katie in love with Tom.
But I didn't know it at the time.
Naked, I rolled over on my belly.
Let my erection subside.
The children finding sand easier to play in.

The water cold.
Tom and I stood on the platform a long time
before diving in, coming up shouting.
I was the first naked, eager for it. Leaving my clothes behind
and running to touch the water for an excuse.

Nancy quiet, the least apparent.
Was the only woman naked after a while.
Was Katie naked? I don't think so.

I was overweight. Alan trim. Tom the one loved.

Tom climbed the wooden tower.
I looked out across the pond, up at Tom,
back for a moment at the others circling around a spot.
Finding a smooth spot for the sacks of food and clothing.
The children. What were the children doing?

I went around the pond. My boy followed.
His sister too small, still with her mother.
Was she ever naked or did she just seem so?

I wanted to be naked, at a distance from the women,
and the men.
Come walking back at them.
Worried about the sharp gravel underfoot.
Looking down, seeing my gentials.
Being seen.
I looked up. They were looking in the sacks for sandwiches.
Still too early to begin eating.

Nancy's large ass.
Patricia with stretch marks. Covered up.
Never uncovered. Sullen.
Alan's closest friend. A dancer.
Tom's wife. Katie my wife.

Terrible things happening.
Children drowning.
Getting lost, being hunted after.
Out by the horses.
Looking for poison oak. Pointing out the poison oak
to the children.
The fog coming in and burning off.
The long view of the artichoke fields
and seeing what adults would do.
What were we doing?

So, reflecting now. From the distance,
Nancy seems attractive.

Alan the sad one. No. I am the sad one. Naïve.
Some sympathy for the cows. Their pond.
Running when Alan yelled. He the expert.
Knowing what to yell.
Seeing a bull. The stray bull.
Missing from someone's farm.
Alan the neighbor. Hunting for the stray.
Warning us off.

I a swimmer.
Tom a swimmer.
The water only a pond. Cold.
Swimming incidental.

We talked. Some naked. Patricia not.
What did we talk about? Katie, my wife,
in love with Tom. I did not know it.
She not noticing that I loved her perspiration
in the sun,
touching a fly off her shoulder.
She was naked.
Her stretch marks not showing or I don't remember.
Yes.
I remember her ass, larger than she wished.
Everyone's about as bumpy and wrinkled.
Her awkward run to the water.
She selfconscious of Tom.
I thought she was afraid to be naked.

She was embarrassed naked in the sauna
with Kevin and Lisa.

I naked, probably the first.
An erection coming quickly.
Sending exhilaration through me. Subsiding.

I can be naked. The first to it.
Still afraid of horses, children, men, women.
Ignored. Katie in love with Tom.
Patricia covered with . . .
her awareness?

Patricia and Tom now divorced.
Katie and me now divorced.
Nancy divorced before. Alan single.
Even Kevin and Lisa divorced.

Not so foolish as to blame the water
or the sun or nakedness
or the children or animals.
We paired every way we could think of.

Nancy seems more beautiful, in memory now.
The rest, now that I know the story, not so interesting.

Tom and I driving by the artichokes stacked in crates.
Trying to buy some from the pickers.
No English.

Leaving the pond because someone came up in a truck,
I think, with fishing gear.

I Direct the Phone Book in a Symphony

I direct the phone book in a symphony
with a short piece of fallen cornice.

The table lamp presides
like a bundle of flaming sticks.

San Francisco tonight is cool
like the outreaches of a campfire.

I am sitting in my kitchen
like a man with connections.

It matters not whether or not
you carefully choose
the rampaging automobiles
you step in front of,
the pain is the same.

When your truck bursts into flames,
and you enlist a farmer to toss dirt
on the miserable event,

When you tell the story
with no love of it,

When you surround
your prairie mud and straw house
with incompetent cavalry,

Of course the Indians
of your true desires
will get in.

My father tells me
he wanted his sons
to lay a thousand bucks a month
on him in his old age.

He's going into his old age
just like I go into the phone book.

Blind hope and blind love
anticipate our blind date
with the future.

Two Letters at Once

My brother writes to me from Illinois where
he is living in our parents' house
''Are you going to send me my pants,'' he says,
and then he describes the pants,
''The blue corduroy pants with the flap on the back pocket''
Then he says he needs them

Then he tells me he ran into my all-time favorite girlfriend
at the country club in East Moline where he is a bartender
And he mentions he met another girl who said I had told her
once she reminded me of an Easter egg

He says he forgets her name
He says my favorite girl friend has two kids and a bald husband

Then he says that Dad and Mother have gone to Mexico
Then he says that he and his girlfriend are going to
Jamaica Jan 8

Then he says, ''send me my pants''

Then he asks me to help get him back into school out here
Then he says he'll be out here in February

He finishes by saying,
''The snow is two feet deep but today is beginning to melt''

Then I open the letter from my friend Chuck who is living
back in New York with his parents

His letter comes to me on a Macy's bag
He jokes around about working at such a humiliating job
as clerk at Macy's

Then he talks about our friend Paul who is in the Yucatan
and how terrific that is
I mean whoever actually goes where they say they want to go

Then he says he's saved up 350 bucks and is about to move
into the city
He says he's expecting a job at one of the 75 private schools
he's applied to

Then he asks me to send him a copy of the play we once
wrote together

and he says he has included a dollar bill to pay for the copying

But I look and there is no dollar bill
I look on the floor to see if I dropped it
I look in the bag to see if he's being cute about it
but there is no dollar bill

So I reply,

''Cheapskate,
I'm not going to send you another goddamn play,
there's no dollar bill anywhere.''

And,

''Fuck you, you bastard,
I'm not going to send you your goddamn blue pants,
I didn't ask you to leave them here,''

And then I,

Zerox the pants
and I send a copy of them to Paul in the Yucatan
who never writes me any letters.

Dear Paul, I Have Got Drunk in Your Honor

Dear Paul, I have got drunk in your honor,
reeling around the passageway, stumbling
between the faucet and the pouring rain,
inhabiting the house with my hands.

I have called everyone I know tonight,
except you, because the Yucatan is unlisted.

On TV, a man convicted of a crime of passion,
reneges before the climax.

I aimlessly piss my lurching desire
into the River of the Porcelain Banks.

Please forgive me if my note is brief.
I am in the city, and here we are discreet.

There's danger in the city.
Its harder and harder to get drunk.
I hear Tequila's fifty cents a quart in Guatemala.

The woman I wrote you about eats and drinks
alongside me.

The town is a desperate place.
I hear Mexico's hot and humid,
and drinking is an acceptable
escape from difficulties.

There's a beautiful episode
of drinking on TV,

A man rides a horse down a road
and there's water flowing in a stream
like booze.

Mexico must hold such wonders.

Ah, The City Smells Like a Forest Fire

Ah, the city smells like a forest fire.
Jim brings Bambi to my side to calm me,
and a charred squirrel to sharpen my fear.

What exactly is
an emergency medical poet?

Why is he carrying bandages
AND a blunt instrument?

Ah, the city smells like fish and chips,
dumped on its victims
like a pile of leaves.

A poet is often the only care available
when the accident occurs,
and he's just as likely
to kick the victim,
as kiss him.

My Friend Flew in from Denver

My friend flew in from Denver.
I hadn't seen him in 11 years, and boom.
On the second day of his stay,
He lay on the couch in an insulin seizure,
his body in convulsion,
his eyes bulging demonically.

I had sent the kids to wake him up,
to go out to dinner.
Jack ran back to my room.
He scares me, Jack said.

He and I went to college together, now
I held him in my arms, bending his rigid
body against itself at the waist,
my hand at the nape of his perspiring neck
pouring orange-pineapple juice and sugar water
between his cigarette-stained teeth
over his swollen tongue.

C'mon, man, drink it.
Swallow, swallow.
That's it, that's it, that's good man.
Beautiful.
He gulped and
swallowed an infant's amount of juice.

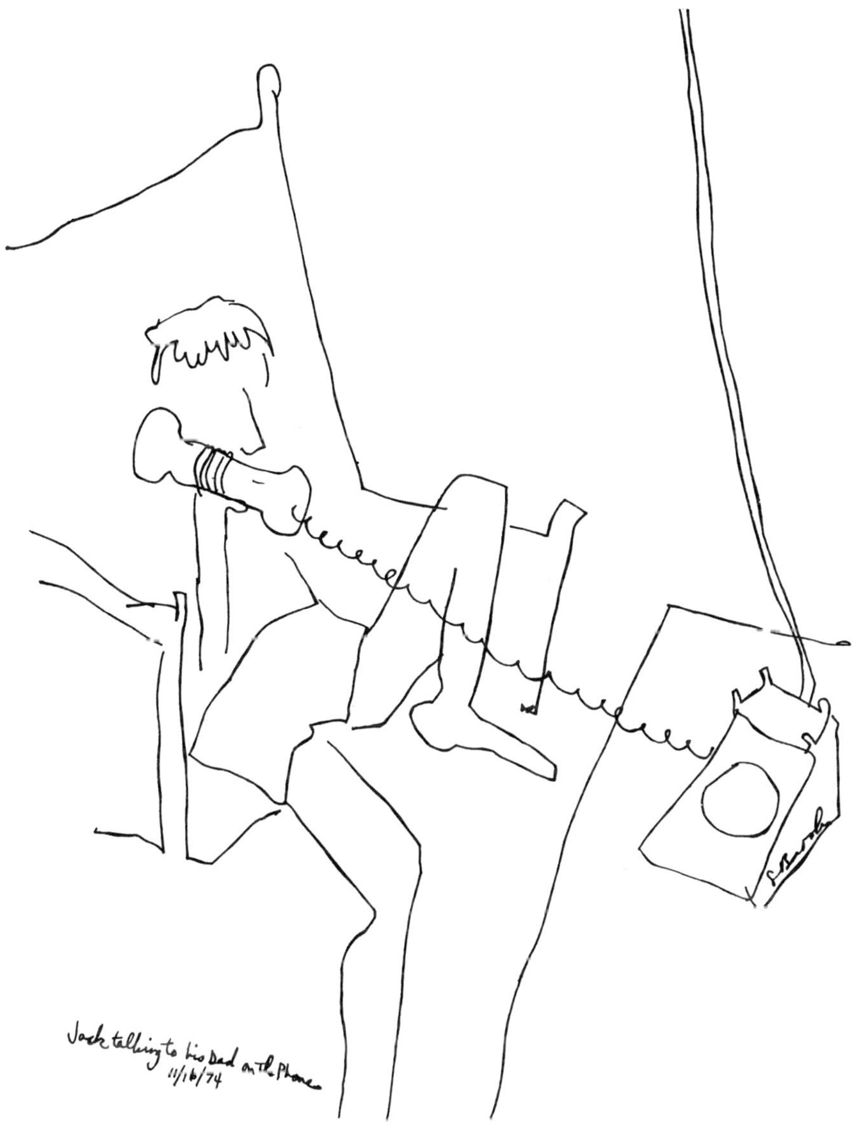

Drawing by Steve Brooks

Bob was easy-going and
droopy-eyed in college.
A year later he discovered he was diabetic.

Rachel, get me a towel.
5 years old, and as soon as I said it,
she handed it to me.

Before he went into shock,
before he went to sleep,
he told me he was a diabetic.
I got a card out of his wallet,
and it said, I am a diabetic,
If I do not respond, If I act strange,
it's because of my condition.

C'mon, he said, almost without consonants,
bug-eyed, gurgling in his throat.
C'mon.
What do you want?
C'mon, he said.
And I was embarrassed.
I thought, He wants me to
hold him, to comfort him.

I had the body of a full-grown man
in my arms and he wanted me
to cradle him,
to nurture him and care for him.

He flew out here
for a job interview.
They gave him 30 minutes
and they ignored him
like an over-eager suitor.

I asked him,
What do you want?
Do you want more honey?
Do you want to rest?
Do you want more juice?
Do you want to sit up?
C'mon, he said, in a
demanding, desperate groan.

The city ambulance drivers stood around
like helpless passersby
masking their helplessness
with first aid information
they recited uneasily
as I held my friend.

In Denver, 10 years ago, he took
me and my brother to the dog races,
and to impress another friend,
he introduced us to Denver traffic
with reckless finesse and called it
a traffic move.

In school, he had missed an afternoon class
for several weeks and it became
a recurring dream of mine,
to have missed something for months,
without excuse, with terrible fear.

He spit mucus and honey,
from aspirating the fluids,
onto the towel.

I wiped his cheeks and lips.
Good, man. Good.
He coughed and groaned,
almost a wail,

he dragged his arms
in the air above his head
and knuckled his eyes
and spit like a comic infant
onto my shirt sleeves.
Thanks a lot, pal, I said,
out of relief.

Seeing an old friend,
with an embrace of recognition,
after 10 years, knowing there was
so much good talk ahead of us.
When a better ambulance came,
they strapped him in and
carried him down the steep steps
like a man down a mountain.

The driver asked me for his details.
33 years old,
College teacher, divorced, alone,
diabetic, tired,
under emotional stress,
away from home,
possible shock.

We had spent the night laughing
and telling stories, full of ourselves,
from one bar to another with Carol Ann,
who said, I'm learning so much about you,
because of Bob.

He lay in Room 5,
ministered to by a tall nurse.
He looked at me, and he said,
Jesus, man, and glanced at the ceiling.
I've done this before.

Everytime I come out of this,
someone says, That's amazing, he said.
They gave him his insulin, and his recovery
was so dramatic and so immediate,
someone always had to see it was
amazing.

We took a cab home and got a pizza,
and I told him how to eat his pizza.
He told me his seizure was a manipulation,
and that I was the one manipulated.
And now I'm telling you how to eat your
pizza, I said, and he nodded.

You know, you're the first person
to tell me they've been manipulating me
before I resented it.

We talked about living analytical and
manipulative lives.
It's layer upon layer, he said.

At breakfast, he said,
You are a performer.
Do you think you are unique in it,
or do you think other people do it too?

I said I thought I was unique,
but I thought everyone did it too.

On a picnic today, he acted out a
two-panel cartoon from the New Yorker.
A cave man held meat over a fire,
while his woman and kids cowered in
the background.
In the second panel, a suburbanite

held meat over a barbeque pit,
while his wife and kids recoiled
in the background.

He enacted the scene with energy,
and made the ground beside the picnic table
a theatre.

He thanked me before he flew home,
and we both knew he'd made something happen
to thank me for,
but it didn't matter.

Jack wore his Cub Scout uniform all weekend,
even though the troop had disbanded,
the den mother had resigned.

Someone at the picnic had called the Boy Scouts
a fascist organization, but I said, No,
it was ritual, it was happy ritual.

Filling Out the Tight Pockets of the Spirit

Filling out the tight pockets of the spirit,
and country music at dawn to pump alive the blood,
thinking about my old bed of soft nails.

TV is no cave entrance,
the flashing horizon of cartoons
is no place to go to.

Dear god, who has no face,
no name, no language,

I want to take it like an animal,
not like a man.

The purgation is weak these days,
the crop dusters are succeeding.

The bugs are getting stronger,
and the plants are getting weaker.

The bugs were doing all right on their own,
look what they did to the Mormons.

Now for a change,
I can hear my heart beating in my ribs,
like a gorilla with gumption.

There are two ways to smoke a cigarette,
one, like a head in the oven,
another, like a tongue in the campfire.

These incisors used to chew raw meat.

There's a conga drum in the kitchen
laughing, mocking the telephone
that sits like a plastic lizard
on the shelf.

The damn red thing
couldn't bite a bison on the butt
if it had a map and an army
to back it up.

Swift was right when he dreamed
the pitted moonscape of the human face,
wrong when he despised it,

No civilized formica,
we are quarries and swamps,
we are caribou,

infested with worms.

We are sharks not submarines,
dolphins not bathyspheres.

Move over monkies,
I'm hot for your jungle.

They're playing music as loud as they can
at 2 A.M. in the Stadium Garage,
and the cars therein move not a muscle,

Neither do they dance,
but the music continues in the night.

Don't Cut Your Hair in Your Ex-Wife's House

The stranger says, one thing for sure, when its crummy
down here, you know its not any better in the city.

She was sitting neck deep on the first shelf of the Jacuzzi,
her body a distorted dwarf in the water.

Do you drink beer, she says,
I'm working as a waitress to get money to be a
chiropractor.

She had been a farm girl, 20 miles from my ex-wife's
home town in Iowa.

I told her I was a poet.
Sounds exciting, she said,
and I dropped the subject.

I'm in 210, she said, drop in for a beer.
Will you be here tomorrow, she said,
indicating the swimming pool.

Its a great place to be a kid,
no hassle and lots of room, you can
leave the front door open,
there are other kids,
rules that nobody cares about,
schools that don't matter,
walls.marbled by hand prints.

No smoking on the pool deck,
the lifeguard is a teenager talking to his
girlfriend.
The rejuvenation of spent bellies is grist
for the mill of lazy uncaring.
Why don't I want to live here and
give up, like everybody else.

On TV, there's Rudolf Nureyev telling Morley Safer
why he won't have kids, it would drive
the little imbeciles crazy.

My ex-wife explains in a diary I find
that I seemed at times during our
''unhappy'' marriage a mundane
and adolescent person, and so I am.

And here is Meadow Oaks,
and Mountain View,
and, I'll take two years at Foothill College,
the future chiropractor says,
it can't do me any harm.

But it is passion I seek,
beyond the comfort.

I fix dinner.
I fix a flat tire.
I fix the adjustment on the TV,
but I can't get a fix on passion.

They're bringing gambling to Atlantic City
to bring the bored-walkers alive.

I will strut my vanity on a stage,
put my larger-than-myself inside
a self larger than me and watch it fit.

I'm trying to get work as an actor,
I like being a poet.
I like my work.

This may be real life down here,
but it's lousy theatre.
It may be conversation,
but the conversation is over.

In the Lovely Half-Light of Late '75

(after Breton)

In the lovely half-light of late '75,
the air is a splendid red-grey from the
Best Foods Mayonnaise factory,
and the forest of toppling buildings I
prepare to enter is
fronted by fire engines
careening into crowds.

I have been waiting for you
to take this walk with me, if
a person can be called
important for love.

The blue sky is diffused with bricks,
and the woodland paths are scattered
with unbroken cemented hearts.

All my illusions are being replaced
because of you.
My children are bringing me cotton gifts.

The Syrup on the Balcony

It is juvenile to wrap yourself in waxed paper
easing the vision
between the plastic case of the newspaper
and the unprinted ''I care, I care.''

Susie is my cousin,
she's a soulful limper
sister,
she's all roses and toeses
and fleecing the lamb again.

Nobody questions the questioner,
nobody makes a piazza out of the most
appropriate noses that demand
it by their availability to the backyards
of the sinus desire that
drips like a questionnaire onto the sidewalk
in front of the innocent who most need
to ask the question and yet they are the very
ones being queried. Nevermind for answers.

The syrup on the balcony makes watching the
parade a slippery affair.
I know better. I saw a longhorn in
the stairwell,
looking for a hotel room full of merchandise,

sitting in the cafeteria downstairs
relocating detonator caps from his
brain to his fingertips.

And yet I feel all giddy like a kid at the
ripply end of a long swing arc,
I don't feel rigid
or geometric,
I feel like running down the corridors
of my vesicles like a wheel chair
like a real chair,
I feel like a flesh and blood, fleshy, bloody,
fleshed and blazing, flushed and brazen,
flambuoyant, brooding, breeding,
flames buoyant,
flicker on the water,
tongue on the lips,

Egg comes out of the shell
like a hope,
like a drambuie of the tasted dream
bowie knife.

A little doggie goes down on the cement
like a noise of a shadow,
like a sight you see when the sound
you hear appears in the
great big cavern of your eardrums,
and you get all wet
in the warm rain that comes down
in the blazing sunlight.

Mama,
I answer with a clean plate.
Mama,
I loved your fried apples, your fried potatoes,
your fried lies.

Mama,
Ask me a heavy question about water,
Today,
I have gotten wonderfully wet,
Mama,
I think there's a swimming pool in
North Beach that I can live in like an
almond in a roca,
like a pinball player in a pinchback suit.

Its true, Mama,
Goodnight, Mama,
Goodbye, Mama,
Hello, mi corazon.

Hello, my most
baby, unbaby, my
every wonder, my
end of it all.

I have finally
come clean like a
crawdad gone thoughtful
on the water close
end of the lakeside sand,

like an armful of arms
that wail in my arms
like I love you,
like I love you all,
like I love you all you are.

Goodnight, Kate.
Goodnight, Irene.

When the moon comes over the mountain,
I'll see you in my dreams.

2

Express Time

Stephen Vincent

☆　☆　　　☆　☆　☆　　　☆　☆

There is a woman in me
who keeps writing poetry.
She won't shut up
even when I tell her
how dangerous it is.
I am her custodian
after all. I have to make
the living that supports
her and she keeps saying
all of these things
that are going to get
me into deep trouble
if I don't hold the line
around her, teach
her there is a difference
between action
and entertainment
and she's breaking that separation.
Her whole cover is going
to be blown and me with it
if she keeps letting this
strange stuff out
about freedom and bliss
and pain and a life
worth living
and if she doesn't calm down
I'm afraid she's going
to start telling me
to shut up
that I'm her enemy
not her protector
that I'm doing more damage

to her than any cop
ever laid on a poet
except a few
who were maybe women
in disguise anyway
and if I don't shut up soon
she's going to put a
dress on me and loads
of makeup and make
me look like some fraudulent
fake and then she's
gonna rip me apart
and tell me what
a real woman is like
and if I were sharp
I better integrate
quick.

Flinching

the difficulties
of being in touch with each other
approximate
my hate for myself

☆   ☆   ☆   ☆   ☆   ☆   ☆

comment c'était?

et puis?

non.

☆   ☆   ☆   ☆   ☆   ☆   ☆

centering

rowing horseshoes zipper fly bra
buttons up
buttons down
buttons wrist
rarely acrosst
kissing mother
kissing father
the date Lincoln was shot
the hour the minute the second
not driving down
the center of the street
walking
backwards
drunk driving tests
on major highways
hitting the keys
on this typewriter
saying the right thing
at the wrong time
I love you
to the elevator
the return home
leaving
disregarding direct shame
surfing motorcycle
driving taxi at night
putting a nickel
instead of a dime
in a parking meter
shoestrings
relaxed neck
approaching a woman
without prejudice
using butter
in an anus
careful dialing
the right number of rings
before hanging up

cautious abuse of superiors
angle muscle release
not flinching
an umbrella in Kansas
sitting under it in a wheat field
mid-day sun July 1973
getting high on an apex
drama drama drama

centering
the all American art
amplified beyond reason
going down the highway
90 miles an hour
trying to find the right song
on the dial
your sweaty thumb
the stations drift
welcome home
as you look for

patience before lurch kiss touch
not waiting too long
right there when you both
want it
or the wait before it reoccurs again

the moral ambiguity
of all contemporary occasions
you meet too many people at once
all so hungry
you so unfed
the lack of depth
in any particular situation
you reach out further each time

52

and what's to stop the thought
of the spectacular
except that it hasn't happened
yet and you keep trying in
subtle or unsubtle ways
to break the perimeter
reach out or box your way in
just to see if you can enter
the red balloon or the blue space
where visions of the secret happenings
of spark plugs over engines
will release release
will give yourself into
that point where the
original explosion will occur
a line will be activated
you will talk across a steady line
up and down the cardiogram
horses will not appear
but you will ride like the unknown
cowboy beneath your radio
you will touch nose breast eye
you will keep it up keep it up
like they promised when you were seven
no gun in hand but the breath
of the listener

and you will sing
sail away sail away as you hop
from horse to boat as the water
comes flowing deep and by
and you dream zebra
as white force meets dark force
and we pull down into
each other
the currents do not reverse
but you play with the
curve shape line
following the sweep

boom boom and you remember
the dance the arc electric
back and forth
you are ten feet away
from each other
but the hands speak tongues
the shape of Italy the dragon
incarnate orange

flows between us
we stop electric

as our bodies
ship into flow

ecstasy the juice
is merciless

it just goes & goes & goes

why are we
so ever
timid
today

First Scroll

There is a margin

The small shatter
The small shattering
The sexual shatter

The hazel nut
in my forehead

You come close to killing
what you leave.
You leave your mother, your father,
your brothers. You are in the kingdom,
kingdom of madness
kingdom of flesh
I always liked the word 'dumb'
in kingdom.

I go flat & dumb
high & dumb
just plain dumb.

The secret of feeling
is that it loves to speak
for itself. It will answer
anybody's call.

☆

The secret of feeling
is that it loves
to speak for itself.
Speech is a lovely residue.
We learn to name to the colors.
Blue green pink
Horror red grey grunge
The animal that carries

55

four colors at once.
Do not name me
Do not name me
Feeling calls out of my mouth
my toes my pelvis
Do not name me
When I come
I moan

I keep saying 'terrific'
when I speak of you
terrific terrific terrific
as if
'ific' is terror overcome
or reconciled. That is
you do terrify me
but the terror
the eyes, my eyes
wide open, the body,
my body, totally open shaking
like a brain dispossessed,
what happens then
that engine roar body feeling
it comes from spinal behind
takes everything
the whole body is rush
towards electric completion
I cannot say anything
it is terrific.

I have not written poetry
for months. I did not want to invent images
for what has happened to my body.
I did not want language to interfere
with growth with the terrible changes

of pulse of thought of whatever
has me into you
and out of you
like a magnet. As I write this
I hear the tone 'hopeful'. And *hope*
you say is a *passive* word something
that goes against the vein
of your body. Perhaps what I really
want to say, what I will say now
is that I was afraid
of your body I was afraid my language
would say I was afraid;
I was afraid what I was not afraid
to have language say
when I was alone when I wanted to
speak terrible truths of my isolation
and loneliness that I did not want it
to say the same things
with you that just the fact
of being with you was
now resolution (just as I write this
I hear you sneeze loud and harsh
in your sleep in the bedroom and my
whole body shakes in fear that
you hurt) & I know that sensation of fear
is exactly our worst enemy
enemy of the body enemy of orgasm
argument or any direct conversation
where I am revealed to a revelation
of your self flowering wilting
or just in trouble. You have planted me
in a long siege of excitement. No. That
is wrong. That is also the enemy. You
have not planted me. I have planted myself.
I have begun to risk the plantation
of self, myself. But somehow it is you
something that you give me, is it
electric animal energy, or nothing so
romantically placed as that language,

but energy energy energy
but that is so simple just to declare
energy cause it is so complex how we
move through each day where we claw,
we hold, we destroy, I can't find the
words that sound new, I could cry for
the use of color, but words that will
not repeat the rhetoric of emotions,
maybe a metaphor, a game of doubles
on a tennis court, where we change
sides, serves, and the squares in which
the first ball must hit to strike off
that battle, *deuce, love,* etc. (you cough
again, I erase the words *deuce, love,*
as just being rhetorical extensions of
the metaphor, and then I cross out this
whole parenthesis as nothing but extension
of thought insidiously designed to thin
the feeling flat).

And I think of our trip down the coast
today. How we had started to just go out
to Sears to get the T.V. repaired and
how the service man estimated it would cost
$35 to $40 and instead of flipping &
getting angry at home for the thing to get
repaired, I said let's go down the coast;
we'll get a pumpkin. But the idea here
is not to tell the whole story. Or just
give some pretty image of orange pumpkins
lying in flat fields with the ocean
and cliffs of Devil's Slide behind,
not that that image could not be carried
as lust or dream or some sweet consummation
of a different kind of love or presence
between two people at a different point
in their lives or just plain fine landscape

painting for the cover of some rich photo-
graph; but the image I carry is much simpler
looking down off the highway riding down
Devil's Slide, the several rip tides
whipping the waves into the cliffs, the
white foam splitting from one point, one
angle to another on enormous dark green
waves the large inward tuck to swell that
takes my eye by surprise sliding it thru
the window like elastic from my two hand
steering wheel grip.

I am just trying to paint that image
not to paint it for the sake of painting it
today that can be done so much better by
camera, by the movie, what I want is to
gather in that energy, the energy that
rolled through my pelvis when we came
back when we fucked
late this afternoon.

When we finished you asked, ''How was it
for you?'', and I said my body was *clear*.
I didn't say that exactly but it's what
I meant that I had been released like all
the tightened structures of pelvis and
arch had been sprung like my body had
been in a trap (like just knowing the
financial torture of Sears Roebuck charging
$41.60, or claiming an hour and a half
labor at $26 / hr plus six dollars
in parts had jammed a piece of my flesh)
or was that moment at Sears really minor
(when we came home there was mail, two
negative and one positive, two overdue

59

traffic violations, and one with my
State tax refund) was my body really
just speaking to you the literal name,
the literal ocean that had filled it
hours before and wanted out, wanted out
of my body back, no, not *back, back*
would imply my body as a dead place and
the ocean wanting to escape, not just
a natural matter of ocean entering
the world of my body feeding it energy
transforming it into physical flesh
movement into the sexual current of our
bodies gathering love.

I like the word ''gathering''
like a spiritual harvest.

But then you pointed your finger
to my forehead and said, ''up there, too?''
And I had to say no, not completely,
there is still resistance and there
was something fighting, or only recording
the movement of the ocean, arguing whether
or not it was right to fantasize about
the oceans, and didn't oceans mean mothers,
and did I want to be a mother when I was
fucking, especially my mother,
or was this vision of the ocean forwarding
all my body feelings really what the expression
''mother fucker'' was all about, not that you
were fucking your mother, but that you had
joined your mother or more than that the
mother of the whole earth, that gigantic
source of energy, the ocean, and that you
were giving it into the shape of the coastline

60

your wife, your lover. And all this goddamn
thinking, how pretty and thoughtful, was
going on, interrupting the flow, interrupting
the flow, those tides ripping back and forth,
as my brain remained tight assed static
position tripod camera up on the coast side
instead of joining the ship
coming home.

And your animal is at war
with my animal for my animal
plays dead and superficially tormented
while your animal is alive and angry
full of lust and kick in the ass
and you kick and you kick and you kick
and my *dead* animal says
why are you so possessive
the way an athlete complains at
the beginning of season the coach is working
him too hard that the demands are too great
and why not go back and sleep the sleep
of warm summer
until finally there is a breaking of air
something hot and sharp slits
down the lung and rips you alive
and your feet love the ground
and the new dancing. But everyday
I say. Must I do this everyday. Can't
I just go out and run
instead of fuck. And your body says
no, run after write after eat after
but don't avoid me
I am the source. Enter me enter me
it is not only for me
it is for *both of us* if we cheapen it
if we pretend it's not there
if we are only

talk around the body
if we do not live through
the body if we do not take the wave
if we do not take the breath
if we do not if we do not
we are not.

& so brain up there
beats the shit out of the body
says you are not shit
you are not piss
you are not breath
you are the thought of it all
& the brain is a bitch, this thing
I must call my brain
is a bitch. It's my mother. It's my
mother inherited. It's my mother The
Planning Commission. It's my mother the
hysteric. It's my mother the concerned
the thoughtful the rational. It's my mother
the fear of the sexual. It's my mother
the Presbyterian. It is my mother sending
four boys to Christian Science Church on
Sunday. It's my mother cleaning our under-
wear everyday. It's my mother vacuuming
the floor everyday.
It's my mother in the League of Women Voters.
It's my mother hating Nixon.
It's my mother refusing to call for fear
she'll find her son ''up to mischief'' that
is stretching his cock into a dark place
she cannot understand. It's my mother with
six cans of Dutch Cleanser underneath the
sink. It's my mother not my mother it's
my mother not my mother it's my mother
not my mother it's the mother in me the
mother I inherit the Victorian petticoat

I wear inside my body it's stiff pink folds
designed to kill feelings designed to let me
into Job's daughters. Lots of luck.

I have killed the morning sun. I have
broken it with my shears. I stare back
into the dark with a bottle full of
empty feathers. I break the bottle on
my head. I break the bottle. I go insane
from the pain it is the first thing I feel
it is the first thing since they scissored
my penis and said ''go home''.

I carry the darkness like the wind. It is
empty and pure. I give it shape with my hate.
I build a mask. The eye brows are as thick
as 2 x 4's, the mouth is a 2 x 6 opened up.
Wood wood my father was a builder of wood.
I build this mask for my father. I give it
patience I give it death I give it every
terrible feeling that I know. My mother
does not walk out against the snow;
she lives in a house she cannot stand. I
build the mask for my father. I deliver it
to my mother so that she will *understand*.
No one understands anything. The house
catches fire and both of them fall. We
are dead dead, dead again. The music is
the pain of a people who have no root
who were bought and killed and then manu-
factured to die.

There is a close and spiritual heart
to all of us. It's impossible to say this
without sounding corny. People do not
want that space invaded whether it carries
agony or something ecstatic like the memory
of love. Anything that causes real tears,
a real collapse in the body, is terrifying.
The fear is that it will be the elimination
of the last piece of private property that
we individually own. If we turn ourselves
inside out the commercial homesteaders
will instantly appear and take it all away
carpet it into vast sentimental profits,
pimp and bastardize what was pure. This
goes all the way down to love making. O
how we moan, how we talk, how we imitate
some rhetoric, some fake motion of loving.
We don't let it come out. *It* might cry. *It*
might be stronger than us. *It* might do ter-
rible things to commerce. *It* might make
pleasure or pain too terrible. too incredible
to yet stand. *It* might do all these things,
and then just say, it's time to go back to
work, or it might just say it's time
to change the nature of your work. Like you
better love *it* just as well. That everything
is connected and that sex is not just porno-
graphic insight but the flow, the energy
we give all our lives and it will drive you
mad if you jam one end
and open the other.

Drawing by Debra McGee

Part Two

She taps away
in the next room
she's a painter
she taps
away
her vision is so solid
but the paper is still flimsy
we buy heavy tacks
to hold it in place
what is it
it is ''transformer''
what is *transformer*
''Transformer''
is a French verb
it means to continually
do it
it means no gesture
is constant
it means we are continental
& life has no mean
except the gestures
we make to fill it
we make gestures
that capture & mock
every moment
of tradition
not only our tradition
but your tradition
traditions don't mean shit·
it means whole countries
are rotten inside
no not even rotten
simply dead apple skin
over which we walk
& gesture & gesture & gesture

☆   ☆   ☆

Actually it's much more complicated.
I was just fooling with
that critical word ''gesture''.
The gestures are serious.
In fact each gesture
is an explosion
carefully manipulated
however not to destroy
the gesture which speaks
back to androgyny
to a passion of contact
to a ritual breather
that was cosmic
& never allowed
the local

☆   ☆   ☆   ☆

tap tap
next door
next wall
you tap
a painting
no color particular
that is yes
there is a particular
color flesh colored pastel
or brown or blue
or banana yellow
but no long careful
attention to depth
as in older paintings
where color was the chief
where color made your heart
go warm
or cold
or cosmic.

today
you make it different.
it's theater
these paintings you make
are theater. They talk.
no. They don't talk. They
make gestures. They explode
without exploding. We walk out
of their presence
either an imitation of their gesture
(this woman with the long cock
or two legs exactly
different shapes
to fit the new cock
or the man up on the wall
who jacks off with one hand
while two cocks wait on his chest
as his mouth / eye slides
into agony (unable to come)
or the man
with vagina looking only slightly
misplaced) gesture gesture
it is a theater
we cannot sit still
it blasts it blasts
you are a blast
half the people watch
in imitation. Is that correct?
I don't know
sometimes I find the people on the wall
down on the floor
like off-slant mirrors.
But other times explosion
explosion you want us to explode
to the tune
of a new rhythm.

''to the tune
of a new rhythm''
o how soft
you would say
how romantic
can you see rhythm
does it have a tune
shut up mister
you've got it all wrong
it don't stand there
it don't stand there for you to watch
to say it goes around like a tune
it doesn't

☆   ☆   ☆

rhythm in the rind

☆   ☆   ☆   ☆

Part *Three*

Tonight I am a message yesterday I was a
and tomorrow you better believe this
blood engine cries like a broken cow

The message is argument we are not
at home with argument we are not at home
with what are we home for
anyway. I travel a deep spine
it curls itself in it forces itself out
it is the motion of a trembling pink space
that says I am

I am angry
the message is
I am angry
if you slit my throat
four weasels walloping out

The message is when I talk anger
I talk my mother I talk her anger
I am righteousness hold the house together
punish the sons the father tighten the bolts
there is a dangerous storm
about to breathe

The message is
learn how to talk to each other fight like
hell come up you are not breathing
there is a burn in your face
I tear the blister off to find the blood
to find what will feed to find I am a cannibal
to find I am feasting on your blood you say
never no not at all I am not your blood I am
not your meat throttle your own ass keep
your own fingers up your own mast
filthy creep.

The message is I cannot resolve the problem
I cannot wake up we stand in front of this
poem like code like cartographers like
we need a machine a periscope to register
the unknown when all we need you know you say
all we need I cannot come up with the answer
o yes you can what are you afraid it will hurt
not go your way leave you out of control
manipulator castrator all these terrible things
we can do to each other
in one lousy second.

The Kitchen

. . . just because I think I am right
and that you have to agree with me
that I am right you will not
stand for it you are screaming this at me
in kitchen standing up, your eye balls
springing forth like fat grenades
the neighbors are out on their back porches
dancing to the energy of your voice
the energy that does not spring out of their
lives (they are talking to each other
like there is an unexpected game in the
coliseum) I'm oblivious to their whispers,
what they say, I'm listening to your voice
drive into my body as sledge, as hammer,
as thought, as position: I listen wide open
to play the dead man, the crucified,
the better, your voice the big nails,
the neighbor's voice the little nails.
O, it all comes in, until I can't take it anymore
I say I hate you I hate you I'm angry
I don't know why I'm angry I don't know
why you're angry I don't know why I'm angry
I wish this kitchen could be a beach vista
of sea gulls fighting over the ocean
that we were just commenting on how nasty
and ugly sea gulls are to each other
how they fight over food, how they pick
at each other, how they are graceless,
how, even in flight, they are muddy
and grey, totally spiteful,
instead of us here in this kitchen
hitting each other up
all smoke and wilting fire
designed to crush the hell out of each other
how when you get angry
instead of responding to the anger
I sometimes jump up to the ceiling

want to record it for literature
say what a liberated woman I'm living with
isn't she wonderful how she sticks up
for what she feels and won't let me
manipulate or fold her into positions
that do not threaten what I think or
know or want to express unviolated.
But you do not think in those terms
you do not go up the wall and laugh
at what we're doing, or say how silly it is,
or jump out of it you keep laying it on
like an iron which says you will hear me
you will hear it right through the skin
to your blood I am not your slave I am
not your slave I am not your slave
this blood I am touching in you
that I am having to whip you to touch
you iron body thin skin fat quick brain
crazy fascist this blood I am touching
in you will live forever
if you can breathe it
not go dead pretend you are a beaten child
someone that has been walked over and ignored
by his mother, brother or father

just listen

O
I could tear you apart
you have shamed me
you have made me feel
ashamed. You have taken the bones
out of my heart. You broke
the house. The bones splattered
all over the floor. He runs
around naked not a fence in sight.
O why do I hate you

when your hatred is so clean and pure
it jumps out
and then you are free again
your body throws laughter
and freedom all over the place
I am so jealous
of that quick capacity.

Pick me up I pick you up pick me up
I pick you up
one of these days
there'll be a mountain standing
in place of a gesture
I won't give up.

Part Four

Debra paints the elegy
calls it ''Requiem For
An American Painting''. It's black,
solid black on the long high
canvas. At the bottom, strings
hang thru rivet holes and are tied
around antelope bones we found
in Utah. They take winged flight
beneath the dark. We wake up
in the night singing our flesh.
Orphans fly over our heads
from Viet-Nam to a Pasture of
guilt. Warm gold bodies bent
and ravaged by a war. There is
a dark space that slaughters
the country. It is calling
the wounded home. It is breathing

down our necks the fear of the next
day. A collapse is at foot, at
the foot of the empire. The Viet-
Nam in the newspaper is growing
black as province after province
is invaded and taken. A capture
is near complete. The forces of
the home land are retaking hold
on the breath of the landscape.
Recycling the munitions that were
designed to kill what was local,
what was home. And here we come
back with the final lonely trophies
the war babies the orphans the
last booty for the suburban home.
Yes the name *love*, the name *comfort*,
the name *security* is invoked to
cover the fact, the fact of *defeat*,
the fact of *failure*, the fact
of *guilt*, the fact that America
does not belong out there
raping the planet. O, it is
so easy to go abstract to destroy
the beauty in our faces.
There is a rumbling in the ground.
What is victory in the East
is killing a claw in the West
breaking its tentacles into a
thousand pieces. Tasteless stupid
technology. What a people will do
for a Toyota, an air conditioner,
for a way to separate the mind
from the body. There is victory
in the East.

> *for Debra*
> *on her birthday,*
> May 2, 1975

Part Five

How do you avoid pleasure:
you talk about it
you run to write a poem about it
you cut off your veins in the middle
of expression
you glorify punishment
you would love to punish
as you have been punished
you wonder if the mail has arrived
you think you should call someone else
get in on a telephone lip
you jump out of your body
into the business of another situation
a meeting to attend
business to perform
obligations to others
students yes
you love your students
children
yes you love your children
typewriter
yes you love your typewriter
rigid jaw straight back that commitment
to others
no jollies no yawyaws no nothing to get out
but out of yourself.

A channel of air moves up and down
my body
it's a contest not to touch the body
if you touch the body
you're it you're caught

someone other than yourself has you
flesh the name is flesh
the crying tear will not fall
flesh
the cheek will not slide
the bear will not hug
do not touch
do not let the air touch
air to flesh fire
air to flesh fire
put out the fire
put out the fire with air
do not touch
I'm a firm blessing.

This morning so beautiful the sky blue
the air cool with winter rush but the
sun bringing down warmth to body
I ran I ran up the hill
I ran up the hill to the park
my body breathing breathing out
the dank air of morning house
where we did not open the windows
wide enough to let the air climb
down our night sleep I run up the hill
the air coming down like water through gutters
the top the flat course running through the
grass round tennis court back on to the grass
breaking the straight line curving into a
circle my arms out like a compass I run
into circle after circle one hand up
one hand down I balance the world the
gravity of touch waves up
waves down I circle for you
I circle for you the body you
my body

Part Six

☆   ☆   ☆   ☆

I do not remember the birth from my father
and mother how their bodies must have
jammed together still breathing down
youth. My father probably recently home
from the Bay where he had been sailing
his boat. My mother in from the garden
where she had been twining ivy up the fence.
Whether it was before dinner, or after,
or just gone to bed, my older brother
maybe listening, getting frightened,
or fast to sleep. But my father, the wind
off the Bay still rubbing his back, the
same way it had pushed the main sail
across the cock pit tacking up
the Channel out in to the Bay,
or back down the Channel into the harbor,
and my mother, the scratch and feel of
garden earth on her fingers, the handles
of the pruners still a firm felt echo
in her slightly calloused hands. I do not
remember the motions of the two bodies
that made me, the path and receipt
of the seed, the explosion of love that makes
the first body grow that the seed flourish.

Coda

In the morning
everything so pure
She leans over the bath
and the scoop of white color
is right out of classical painting
so red so rich

And I was just passing
down the hall way
to watch the two cats
curl and fight
in the bedroom
the loaded whine
of their little engines

Cats in the bedroom
Debra in her bath
Stephen at the typewriter
a warm morning in November
a splash and a pass.

3

Harness of Bone

Beau Beausoleil

Night Train

And when the night train
is coming in
filled with silver needles

And when the night train
is going down
the vein of every track

And everything is pulled
after it
And everything is pulled up
and back

And when that happens
any number of
hard surfaces soften

And when that happens
there's no money
to sleep with
No money even to rub
the dust from

And when that happens
I cup my hands around
the dwarf star
of my heart

My hands cup below
the numbers that open
in my flesh

And the shadows
in my mouth
burst into fire

And the night train
comes up from the track
running its red light between us

And the night train is all
ivory white in the shade
of the moon

And when that happens
one of us is dead
and the other is in the
eye of the needle

And when that happens
we have paid for the
animal to die
And we have thrown out a
smooth rope for rescue

Under the Roots

In those days
the animal was
killed differently

We turned its blood
a dark blue in the air
above our heads

We rubbed the
hard salt of its body
against our sex

Each vein of the animal
was cut away
and woven

The head was hollowed
and then given back
its voice

We danced and let
the animal leave
its dream

We dropped its meat
far down our throats

Then we called
to the soft eye
of the moon

We sang and
the two sides of
our mouth opened
truthfully

The animal was
killed again

The moon moved
down behind us
and gave the sharp
cry of a dog

We slept and when
we woke
the sun was caught again
in our trap

The Mistress of Captain Kaoru

The snow has written
a graceful character
on the mountain
behind her

This woman
goes in the water

This woman
goes through the forest

Her hair is tied back
with tall grass

She walks like
a samurai

The yellow leaves
are pointed
at her face

This is a clear morning

The gates
are open

She makes
a good sound

Her silks
are red

She draws
her sword

The sun puts

her shadow against
a clay pot

The enemy moves
like a lizard
before her

The dance is easy
the wound comes
through his side
like smoke

His rice will
taste good
in the forest

The screen she
puts around his body
depicts the arrival
of a special friend

The Shark And The Swimmer

The shark and the swimmer
prepare for sleep

They lie on top of the water
their bodies shining against
each other like rough stars

The swimmer's brain
fills with smoke

The milk in the shark's
belly catches fire

They are farmer
and lover
in a quiet field

The farmer biting
his lover
just above the heart

The shark touches
the face of the swimmer

The swimmer joins
with the shark's body

They are dry fish
then red fish
then a tongue
that wakes and sleeps
with the same appetite for life

Father

I was real high up
in heaven

I could see you
my father

It was not sleeping
or drunkenness

I was real high up
in heaven

You said
Go and build

us a house

You shook my hair
as a father does
his son

I went and built it
with the wind all
close together at
my back

Let us eat
and cover ourselves
you said

We ate
drank
We lay down
making up songs

And it was not sleeping
or drunkenness

There between us
was a river with
a boat on it

And we swam to
the boat and cast
out nets

And the day passed
below us in the shape
of a fish

And we caught
the fish and
the river ended

And we left blood
so that the people
could see that we
had been together

And we stepped
from the boat
You into heaven
And me into this
one song, singing
it through the night

Farming A Dead Thing Under

This dead child
was never wicked

She was like the
flame of the holy
candle

Now she is heavy
and filled with a
useless quiet

Now someone
is eating

Someone else
is fixing a meal

Now the Mother
Of God will feed her

We say a prayer
to warm her face

A prayer to rub
the dead with

This day we are
dressed to meet
the priest

This day we will
go up his hill
and speak to his
black hair and shoulders

We will leave something
on his table

I am
a quiet man

As quiet as
my thumbs

This is a
hard time for me

This land seems
to grow nothing
without some sacrifice

Even the sun
hesitates

Even the seeds
must be talked to

Now the dogs will
be barking for
a few hours

And my wife
and I will sleep

In another day
or two the rain
will make a noise
on the ground and
something will grow
here

Falling/Catching

I was seeing you
in the darkness

Green color and
red eating color
were on your face

I was swimming
among the bitter fish

You had many
good fish
they leapt from the sea

No man was near you
You called out for no one

I was afraid then

I went away
and saw you
in a different place

A bird was
landing on your arm

You were whistling and
trading talk with it

It was a bird whose flying
I had always feared

I called to you

Your hands were
gathering food

I was in the blackness
saying only the dead things
to keep my body together

You were speaking,
I think

Then you were cutting
tongues

Then you were cutting
and giving us each
a special fish

Then you were flying
Then I was flying

Then morning colors
were below the trees

Then all I saw were
your eyes and in them
a clear reflection of the light

A Little Ways

The man
went up
a little ways

The woman
went up
a little ways
on the other side

They went up
like water
through a root

Like the sun
they went up
around their faces

The birds
pulled in their wings
and fell down
past them

The fierce animals
rolled over and showed
their bellies to the knife

Everything grew
in a husk

They were opposite
the dead

The man
The woman
They went up
They lived there

Between Us

This is from
one side of
a face

This is a blind

This is the end
of a letter

This is the hitchhike

This is a bowl
of ruby soup

This is paper and glass

This is the hitchhike

This is the tongue
getting out of the way
of the teeth

This is a comb
This is the skin
around your eye

This is the radio dial
This is the insect bite

This is a job
This is an amount
of money

This is a test
This is swollen

This is finished
This is sticking out

This is the hotel
This is the elevator

This is a sign
of life
This is stiff
This is the parlor

This is a drum
This is your shoulder

This is the sun
like a white fan
it opens this room

You appear
to be sitting

You appear to
close an eye

This is a whistle

This is one person

This is spit

This is dangerous

News

The married arson
agreement is over

The five sides
of the one thigh
have been cut

The boiling water
and the two and seven
traffic are backed up,
are at their highest point

You and I are
owned by the mob

The lobster is
on the table

The downtown traffic
is trapped downtown

We represent
two heads
and a child

A child with notes
and numbers on his skin

And a language

A language that runs
back and forth

And a dog

A dog that bites

Thanksgiving

A storm
on the sun

A rolling away
of stars

Under this floor
it is beautiful,
the shoulders of
this house crisscrossed
and strong boned

The house carrying
us quietly like
a knife in a pocket

The house aware
of the hammers

The house aware
of the nails in the
honey of its wood

I play at lifting you
to the highest window

I ask you
what you see

I ask you what
you feel while your hair
twists out of its knots

I eclipse the light
with your body

This means nothing

The farmer putting
in another crop

The necks of some
wild turkeys snapping
on the concrete

The knuckles of
someone bleeding

The shooter putting in
another shell

This festive
time of year

This thanksgiving

Feel This Again

Bring me
the white dog

What I want
is mine
I will stroke my cock
I will stroke her hair

The bitch

Her pregnancy will
have my eye

The child will confess
its love for me

Bring me
the one I've chewed on
the one with three legs

My hand is
a gun

My hand is
a mirror that
looks behind me

Bring me
the one whose eyes are
a fist of blue suns

She disappears

Let me tell her
what I feel now

She reappears

Let me try to mount
her again in the dark
of this room

She escapes

She leaves blood at
the end of my stick

She shows her teeth
and bite

She shakes until
I come loose

A lovely white dog
A bitch

She touches herself where
her scent is still strong

She goes up
on her legs
This woman

She disappears
She reappears

She escapes

Muse One

Hers' is the skin
under which the
clouds of night
gather

She is there
when the blood
finds the wound

She is there when
the bone stiffens

I have seen
the flowers across
her back

The red lace
of her hands

The brown lacquer
of her eyes

She lifts
her arms slowly

The cold water
in her throat

her lips
her teeth

Hers' is the rich
stillness of the
dead animal

Hers' is the cunt
filled with seed

Hers' are the breasts
with milk
for the wild dogs

She has lived
this long

She has lived
in every combination
of the word

She can open
any mouth
and taste it

She can tempt
the truth out to
the very edge
of the tongue

The diamond
I show you
is one poem

The knot I tie
around your neck
is another

Catching Fish

The California coast
is dark

All the knives and
the forks are sleeping

All the cheap legs
of the street
are in the air

I am a fisherman

I come this close
to the water to curl
my arms around the
tide and wait

I wait for the
thick space under
this boat to shine
with veins

I wait for the water
to bring its lips up
to me, so close that I
can cut myself a kiss

I am a fisherman

I talk to
the water

The fish listen
to my lies

I pull the fish
like leaves from a tree

I pull them like knives
from my body

In a dream
the bait slides
down my throat

The hook stands
upright in my mouth

I am a fisherman

I catch fish

My hands swell
as I clean the fear
from them

Nut House

We see above the dark
We dream this color

They send us here
like telegrams
saying

This one thinks
one arm is blood

This one thinks
one leg is shining

This one holds
one arm like a wing

This one moves one leg
in a terrible wish

We go first
to the table
And then to bed

We fall asleep
when all the locks
are motionless

In the morning
they go into us
like seed, like looking
for money they had lost

They want our lives
to go faster

They want us to
spit out a bone and
then remember it

These people sharpen
against our mistakes

They argue with
electricity

The last thing they allow
to come this far is a rain
that falls on your face like
a single strand of hair

I see myself

I see what is sweet
pulled from me

I go to death
on myself

I whirl my arms and words
and they think I
am asking for trouble

Sleeping With Stolen Horses

We were drinking

We went up
into the meadow

The horses were Goddamn
beautiful, they were like
great patches of black
snow on the ground

We rode them down the
side of the hill, we
never thought of goin'
no further but they were
runnin'

They were runnin' like
a dog's dream, they were
starting to sweat against
our legs

Goddamn
It was like findin' money,
it was like with a woman,
nothing was the same,
everything looked different

We rode all day,
some of us got cramps
in our legs

We rode that night
until the horses couldn't
run no more

We got water and something
to eat near here
We slept with
the horses

We meant to bring
them back in the
morning

We never thought
of them as stolen

We were all just
men and horses
runnin' at the same time

Them horses as much
as gave us that ride

We never jumped up
and took it from 'em

Look how far we come
and never looked behind us

We never hurt no one

We meant to bring
them horses home
this very morning

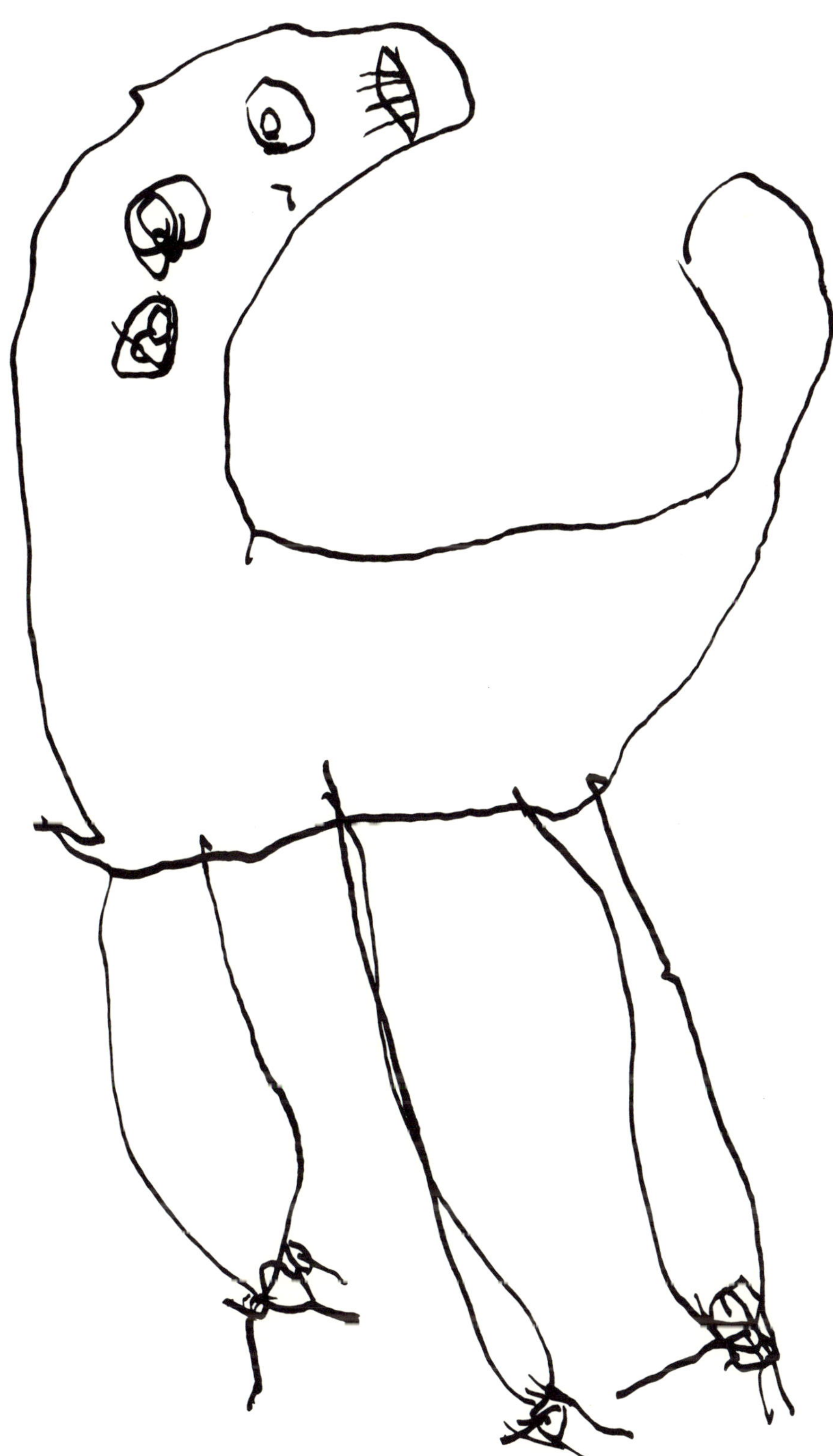

Drawing by Connolly Beausoleil

Water Fall

There are ships
sinking in
the forest

There are ships
sinking

Ships filled with
shifting cargo

Ships with running
lights that equal
the stars

There are sailors
whose necks are
the color of tobacco

Sailors drowning
between the wild
closeness of the trees

There is the braided
hair of the lowering angels

There is the voice
that moves
like a wave

There are the animals
that take ghost steps
across the ground

And finally, there is
the great anger of
waking without sleep
in a dark wood

Thursday

1

I have forgotten
who is dead

I have dreams
of water

Dreams of blood taken
out by hand

Dreams of your white
mineral shoulders

2

My father is dead

He went back for
his coat and every bit
of light on his face
exploded

Sometimes I feel him
lying over me and that

feeling is of one covered
with ashes

Sometimes I feel the same
wounds as the animal
that killed him

   3

I sit with my mother
and we name names

We throw voices
We move lips

We try to see
through the air

Help me,
we cry out almost together

I have forgotten
who is alive

White Mist

My hands
come to you
in the shape
of an animal

My hands carrying
fire wrapped in a
leaf

My hands shading
the ground

Oh, Mother
give me the bright food

turn it towards
me now

Oh, Mother
pass down my body
like the rain

Oh, Mother
put me inside
your color

This mask
I am wearing

This likeness
of three animals

A place I am
seeing

A bear
I am calling

Oh, Mother
open your jaws
and there will be
an offering

Under The Fascists

At night
the deep artery
of the sun
is cut

The smallest light
is taken out

And when we
close our eyes
the night is allowed
to be there

And when we sleep
our lips turn to wax
and we make it worse

Watch the motorcycles
graze like powerful sheep
on the concrete

Watch the cross streets
Watch how the cars
let each other go by

Now we begin
a new month

A new apple of blood
appears in our mouth

We are pigs
selling bacon

We are steers
wearing butchers'
aprons

Another flight of stairs

The stars rise
to the ceiling

The man on
the sidewalk
The woman
crossing the street

They understand the work

It is all blood and flesh
concealed until the knife
reveals it

It is moonlight
and streetlight,
the plain fire
of the sun

We are going
over and over

We begin
to bleed

We begin
to sing

We begin to spit
a clear soup
that feeds us

This extra bone

This shining bone

This bone that walks
through our blood

on its own white legs

We are under the Fascists

We are under the night
until we sacrifice its darkness

Take Off And Be

Your own people
want to find you

Inside
every muscle blisters
and turns again

The memory regains
consciousness

The ink separates
into images and blood

You breathe without losing
the close air around you

You heat your memory
with movements of the hand

Look and see
the ghost in your face

Look up
and see all the words spinning

See them
as stars

Now they fall down
the sides of the pen

They glisten in a pool

You have the lips
of a dead priest

Your own people
want to find you

Terms #2

The moon slides out
and after it
the bone slides out

The stars
stop in the dark
and arrange themselves

To love someone now
is to sail the ship
away in the bottle

To love someone now
is to understand how
the diamond is formed
under great pressure

See how it works

The night falls first
above the shadows

The heart slides out
and after it
the beast slides out

To love someone now
is to close one hand
and open the other

To love someone now
is to understand that
the sun burns itself up
for light

Passage

The light is liquid
The light is sacred

I want to bring down
the sun in perfect darkness

I want to see the blood
that runs its face

Once and for all

I want to carry the body
and kiss it

I want to untie
its knotted throat

A woman is crossing
a field in perfect darkness

She is carrying a bone
that brushes against the sky

Once and for all

The cars are crossing
the bridges like horses

The machines are
rubbing against our legs

The body goes down
into perfect darkness

The body is lowered to
a starting place

4

Moving Day
Hilton Obenzinger

Landlord

A year, a winter gone,
another splattering on,
and still the roof leaks,
15 buckets laid out
down the hallway, on the bed
each storm weeping into my sheets
like the Virgin Mary of Plaster.

Landlord, you stall & blubber,
excuse yourself
for being a creep
in possession of keys
to roof & 4 walls
that are mine, not your deeds,
and are mine to be dry
even as I sleep.

My rent is due
but more so is yours,
even as you smile with the teeth
of Teddy Roosevelt
charging up the steps
to twitch for $275.
I must groan you own
my home
& now myself I must excuse
because I hate paying to drown
my only real
estate.

Evict me! Crucify me!
I'll use my cross
as a giant thumbtack
in your forehead
to post my notice.
I'll leave only when I'm dead
& you can't afford the loss.

Like Luther, I slam
my theses down:
''Landlord,
thou lordest over us now
with a mask of benign power
yet cannot hide your face
of arrogant, incompetent crime
Take a long hike
through the Wilderness.
Your time's up.
We will not kiss your ring.
This House is on

Rent Strike!''

Lamentations and Determinations

Last time I went to Pecwan
more exactly, Klamath River Extension of the Hoopa Indian
        Reservation
(Yurok Tribe)
I went with Pam & we drove along the river
the familair cranky & crooked road
to see the Simpsons.
Night, finally, when we drove in
surprised to find maybe 25 cars parked
askew in the dirt ruts by the coop or down closer to the river:
Must be some party, we thought, sitting in our own dark vehicle.

Nervously we climbed the stairs to meet Hunsucker
who told us Cindy got drowned in the river
2 days before & they had all come to drag the river.

Still abundant Klamath of eel, trout, salmon,
even mammoth sturgeon lurking on bottoms
like succulent aquatic pork;
Klamath, still the old center of universe, the juncture.
We turned to lean on the balcony of the A-frame
to look at it,
trying to see how far
we stood from it.

Barnfires kept watch on the bank all night.
She'd been swimming as she'd done 14 years
dove in, her skull cracked a rock
& Vicki couldn't hold on to her hair, then she was gone
into the current
after the first bob up.

My student, among other things.

I peeked at her 7th grade doodle in her desk
one day before school began
a nosey principal
"Why must our people be in pain . . .
INDIAN POWER . . . Love Peace Love . . .
Don't you think Tiger O'Rourke is *such* a bully?

The river isn't as sentimental as I am, nor even so mean.
The river isn't a typically schizoid 7th grader either
tho now it seems she *is* the river,
a hitchhiker, enrolled in a new school, etc.,
yet the people won't leave the river alone with its catch.
This was no Ophelia or Mary Jo Kopechne, just a quick dunk,
as her life was in the first place, or yours,

suddenly deciphered like a secret telegram
in a shredding machine.
The men cruise, very quiet as a result of determination.
All the people brought food the women cook up,
endless batches, and discuss
equally endless exegesis of
what it was that made God angry at Cindy.

A year before, when the river came close
to a foot of the road
the rains abruptly ceased. We knew we'd be dry
that season.
No houses would float out
in the grayish-yellow, massive, uncanny river,
as in the great flood of 1964
past Requa by the sea
where Oregos, the old round rock outcrop at the mouth, looms ou
informing the salmon what the weather is
or if it's the right time to spawn.
People drove out to the bridge over Pecwan Creek to celebrate,
wine passed around. The white preacher & a visiting evangelist
were in a dingy navigating a giant eddy
away from the swifts, grappling huge logs
for the venerable full-blood who lived at the mouth of the swollen
    creek
to use as firewood.
Pistols out, we took pot-shots at drift
ever so often cutting close to Bjorke's dingy.
"Yahoo! Shoot the preacher!"
Tho nobody did. It was all laughs.
God isn't angry at Cindy.

Just before Thanksgiving vacation
we stood out front washing our car
getting set for the long weekend in SF
when a parent barreled up in his truck.
He reeled out drunk, demanded
of Pam that his 2nd grade daughter
get homework, lots of it

& that I get a haircut, despite the fact
that I cultivated short hair
''Git a haircut or I'll kill you!''
I talked circles, but he persisted, hinted at the gun
in his glove compartment, offered me wine:
''You fucking hippie!'' then blubbered,
sobbing, **''I can't be no fucking hippie,**
      I'm an Injun!
I'm a fucking Injun!''

Lil had them in a washtub
a hundred or so—talking—all the while grabbing them,
slicing their lengths down the middle,
eel-blood sloshing up the galvanized sides, up her arms,
a broad grin as she gabbed.

Ollie's mom was very old, was reared by her grandmother
in the old way in the woods;
refugees from a massacre,
whenever they'd see *waugay* they'd flee.
Others, as children, could remember seeing the smoke of
the old ones across the river or beyond hills.
The story was passed on to Ollie's mom
of when the first whites came.
The Yuroks were aware the whites were down by the sea building
      houses.
As they were having a major dance at Pecwan Creek
word came from scouts the whites were sailing up river.
The festival broke up as they all
rushed to the banks—
it was pointed out to me at which bend—
to watch the boat sail by,
and as it did the wind came up,
capsizing the boat
& drowning those first premature invaders.
After Charles Manson inflamed the press,
Ollie's mom wouldn't talk to me anymore,
insisting I was the devil, that I was a hippie
& all hippies kill.

Imperceptively, word came up from the banks next morning
they got her.
Immediately, the teen-age boys heaved picks & shovels
in a pick-up & went to dig her grave;
her girlfriends in a hush went to prepare her room
for the mourning;
a truck came up, we knew she was inside,
& behind it, in single file, the men walked.

August 1973

Bless the Beasts

for Beatrice

Come morning
we close the cottage door,
lemon verbena bush
in your yard
splattered like a delicate
car wreck;
        lemon verbena
in your hair,
         swinging
like the arms
of a busy population;
lemon verbena abdomen;
lemon verbena vagina—
so hushed
we can walk without
talk, cherished
lemon verbena silking
its way into gulfs,
goals submerged,
          urged
into a tender facet,

our legs,
            4 branches
cut to atomize
our smell casually
across our faces
8 AM
as we walk down the street
mute,
            watching the hills
blink
or the trolleys
freshly tossle their tracks.
I notice the movie marquee
across the street, it says:

**LOVE AND PAIN
BLESS THE BEASTS**

Bless the beasts.

New Year: NYC: "Don't Look Back"

for Phil Lopate

Crosstown bus
a young tan woman
fucked up
sits beside me, hunched
repeatedly offering her seat to a black woman
who demures, keeping her distance
until doubled-up young woman
yells, "Know whatta Puerto Rican?
I'M BLACK, GODDAM BLACK!"
then crawls on hands & knees
as bus bombs thru icy Central Park
muttering, *"My keys
lost my apartment keys . . . my keys,"*

older kinfolk & a young PR triad
of concerned mother, stalwart father, little son
inconspicuously notice

After a day
watching Phil teach video to elementary kids—
José, cameraman,
at 3 PM school-out time
grabs the mike & howls, dances
waves his arms, careens
ecstatic
the big star, the cameraman
who learned to zoom
& focus today—
Phil & I walk down the street
we see a middle-aged white woman
bark, ''Don't touch me, don't go near me
Keep your hands to yourself''
to an imagined but real sexual assault
''KEEP YOUR SHITTY SECRET SERVICE HANDS OFFA ME''
Phil turns to look,
our animated giddy-yap life-talk
cut, he trips over a brownstone stoop, sprawls
headfirst, picks himself up,
plunges on, continues, when
an old man, world-weary & street-wise
never out of step & in low key
advises *''Don't look back''*
& passes

NYC 1 / 74

I Don't Want The Word "Capitalism" In My Poem

I don't want the word
''capitalism''
in my poem. Paper
is getting scarce, energy
too. Poetic
inspiration goes
blackmarket. This
paper is getting expensive.
What I say better be
true.

I'd like to say
''The onions of the moon
stink up the breath
of the night.
My fingers smell
of old telephone
mouthpieces''
but the word ''capitalism''
enters my poem—
even if I reek
of love: ''Capitalism''
robs me even of
my funk.

In the morning
I can see
the Bay Bridge droop
like over-stretched
underpants elastic:

''Capitalism.''

My arms whirl
like tank treads,
my heart bleeps:

"Capitalism."

I never made up
the clumsy word, I
take no credit.
It's not *all* of static,
but it jams our
waves repeatedly,
monotonously.

I don't want
"capitalism"
in my poem. But it's
here, even at
breakfast,
doing charades
of the Titanic
sinking into a
coffee-cup.

Language Lab Sex Struggle

Language Lab SF State:
sophisticated electronic gizmo
practice in
         necesito estudiar
español
      rows of sound-proof
white-pocked cubicles,
ultra-private niches for young souls
to twiddle thumbs
or dawdle between vowels—
and there, on private walls
in this private place
open both to men and women,
graffiti of all the modern

132

great sexual struggles:

Jesus is the pansy from Palestine

Women's Lib may hate me for this, but I must
confess my love for catering to men. Libbers
are disappointed females who just can't
make it. But the blame is not all theirs.
Look at all the dippy guys around. Sometimes
I don't blame them.

FUCK THE SISTER WHO WROTE THIS, SHE'S BEEN CONDITIONED

I tear my earphones off
& duck low in this free-fire zone
to read a tender lyric:

All that is necessary
for women to be free
is for men to become
sensitive to the needs of others

Then, a conciliatory homily:

Treat your old lady
like you'd treat yourself
& everything will be
cool
Treat her better, and
she'll make it up to you

DON'T COUNT ON IT

*Does anyone know where I can get
my hands on a nice pair of breasts*

YOU CAN'T HAVE MINE, *EVER!*

The cassette's run out, I'm set to go
when a sad request is made, and strongly rejoined:

    I would like to carry
    on a continuing dialogue
    with a female because
    I've never known one in
    my life. I'm 18 and think
    it's about time.

    HI, HONEY—
        WHAT DO YOU WANT TO TALK ABOUT?

Baby Welcome

(for Sasha, b. 7 / 9 / 74)

"In Trinidad packs of dogs roam wild
thru streets. In the newspaper
the city hospital complains that dogs
are getting into garbage
from the surgical room, carting off
innards & cut limbs," Kathie says,
explaining the problems of small pet
over-population & her own desire to be a vet
as she suckles day-one babe.
I like the baby & would like to give
a pep talk to that blurry rash
on her nipple:
           "Kid, you're starting over,
this is your chance to make good!
Just remember on your birthday
the great victory of the Australian
working-class vs. Frank Sinatra
& you'll do OK.
        See,
Frank Sinatra comes to Australia

& insults reporters, calls women reporters
'$1.50 hookers', so all the unions
go out on strike against Frank Sinatra.
No stage-hands, no gas for private jet,
no room-service for martinis, in short
he's up shit creek until he apologizes
to the women journalists of Australia
even tho one goon wraps a telephone cord
around a photog's throat & mutters
This is gonna get physical . . .' "
Baby, I look at you, squashed against
Kathie's nipple, & I know you're
flesh of the next wobbly gyrations around the planet.
I just want you to know that Australia
welcomes you in with unwitting grace
& I too welcome you in to the zigzag course
of life & death struggle.
By the time you read this Frank Sinatra
will be a rotting heap in the arms
of Bob Hope, & I'll be wrestling
with angels of naked Boeing 747s
making my own pact with doom.
You were born on a day of one small victory.
Take it from there.

Reeeee-development

Reeeee-development

Hot shit, here come the tractors

Burgers. Colonel Sanders.

Re-shingle old flats,
jack up the rent 100%.

Reeeee-development

24th St:
Instead of Nicaraguan Earthquake Relief Office
McDonalds
Instead of La Raza after-school tutorial program
Kentucky Fried Chicken.

Hot shit, here come the BART
''mass'' transit
funneling in oogling suburbanites:
''We want to maintain the Mission's
quaint Latin ambience—
even a few genteel hippies.''

''—Isn't that charming
how they converted that ugly old factory
into a combo sauna-taco-boutique!''

Reeeee-development

''San Francisco has a tremendous future
as the HQ of West Coast finance,
Capitol of the Pacific Rim:
of course, we need room for secs,
execs, mods, etc.
so a little urban lobotomy
just gotta be. Sorry, folks.
WE GOT PLANS. MOVE!''

Reeeee-development

16th St. wino prophet murmurs:
''Ground zero is right here''
points to his heart
''I don' understan'
yr telegram . . .''

Reeeee-development

"". . . it's finger-lickin' good . . .""

NO WAY!

Sole Support

"Whenever I get close to someone
to reveal my true thoughts
they get MAD—
so I think
love is like buying and selling:
I offer goods which you like
and so you buy.
Yet, if I offer something
other than what you like
you won't buy,
so
I'm careful not to offer
what I know you won't like . . .""

**"DO YOU REALLY
BELIEVE THAT SHIT?""**
I hotly interjected.

"See, that's *just* what I mean . . .
I won't talk about it anymore.""

Old Folks ARE At Home When They Take Their Anger Once Again Into The Street

On the Wells-Fargo bank line an old black man
nudges his one-eyed white partner,
says, ''They all a bunch a crooks
I tell yuh, something's gotta
CHANGE!''

In the B-B-Q ribs joint
an old white codger
tells his Palestinian friend,
''Those boys can't come home,
exiles in Canada,
just like you, cause a that war
& the most biggest criminals
trot around like hyenas, free!''

I ride the Mission trolley-bus
reading ''Workers World'' & wishing it was
when a vigorous grey sage taps my shoulder:
''I see you're reading a radical paper.
Tell me: What ya think of this whole mess?''
Hmm. I say, trying not to overstep my bounds:
''People gonna get together, turn some things around''
& he replies:
''Well, the founding Fathers said we got 2 ways:
either we vote em on their ass
or we make a revolution
& GODDAMIT WE'RE GONNA MAKE A REVOLUTION!''
& we exchange winks.

Or the old Yiddish rootless
cosmopolitan riding the NYC subway
IRT Uptown, who comments,
when 2 po-
licemen walk into the train

& tower above us like blue Himilayas
''Oy! Is dis car
SAFE,'' smacking his cheek & swaying side to side
as we clack into 42nd St in half-empty car.
''But the kveshjun is:
ARE YOU SAFE?''
& he raises forefinger in Talmudic
judgement while the 2
pigs freak out & flee to
next car.

I wonder:
Old folks ARE at home
when they take their anger
once again into the street.

Old folks.

Someday I'll be wise with strength
like them.

Out of Gas

for Robin

Up the hill I run out of gas
& fall back down
to find a space empty
in which to park my
gasless sorrow.

I look out
at the trees in the park,
knobby trees,
which look like skinned
knuckles.

I'd love to sit
& watch these trees
punch out
skyscrapers,
but we've got
things to do.

Robin stays behind
to guard the car
against wary cops
as I seek gas.

& I think:
> *Love is
> embarrassing. I'm
> afraid to touch
> my oozy parts.
> Yet Robin plops
> into my feelings
> like a seagull
> even as I act
> the sandpiper
> scampering back
> & forth, edgy
> at the surf.*

I think:
> *the site of the
> Boston Tea Party
> is now filled
> with garbage
> over which an
> expressway runs;
> we have to dig deeply
> to get at history,
> at life, at
> even love's
> petroleum.*

I love you, Robin,
& I'll be back,
my knuckles around
the gas can.

This is my love
poem. At least
my poem
won't run
out of gas.

Poem for Boys

In the park
up the slope
              I climb
& over the brushy crest
to see over that vista edge
the quick ghost of
a stadium,
              the extended Greco-
bowl of Polo Grounds,
empty & still.

Suddenly 100 cross-country racers
boom out of a hole in the ground,
a tunnel thru bare bleachers—

I stumble closer, dazed,
to be sole spectator
as Junior High boys
huff around the track,
each, as he nears my curve,

straining to the test,
long-distance, in shorts
& sleeveless shirts, numbers tacked on,
black boys, yellow, white,
rasping out serrated lungs;
& each,
   upon seeing me,
plays to his
    lone crowd,
his single judge of manhood
sweat,
   with puffed chest,
chin jerked high, a glance
in his trot, an appeal,
a proud, gigantic gift
     to me
(despite lurking distant Gym Teacher),
a skinny kid's wheeze in the Great Race,
as 100 boys round the bend
& plow into yet another dank
& poignant hole in the ground,
their exit,
leaving the huge stadium
just as suddenly empty & blank once more.

SF, Golden Gate Park, 1 / 74

Percy Bysshe Shelley Is Better Than Hilton Obenzinger

Percy Bysshe Shelley is better than Hilton Obenzinger.
Hilton Obenzinger is a character in a Jack Kerouac novel, like
 Rheinhold Cacoethes.

It's like I absolutely had to be a poet—Hilton Manfred Obenzinger—
with 3 names and no place to put them except down on a blank page.
I'm glad I don't have to carve it in a tree.
It's not right if I blame all my troubles on my name
nor is it right for me to deface trees.
I'd like to see the stone-cutters face when he hacks out my
        tombstone.
With a name like that I'd never make it as a politician.
I'd probably do better as a shoemaker or a poet.
I feel great affinity with Chidiock Tichborne, an Elizabethan poet
who got his head cut off for plotting against the Protestants
& wrote a poem about it which is worth at least the name.
I'll remember to write a great poem before I get my head cut off.

It's the least I can do.

Your Personality May Be Killing You

At the check-out counter of the supermarket laden with fruit &
habitual chocolate cake
I see the cover of Reader's Digest on a rack.
It tells me ''Your Personality May Be Killing You''
& on page 78 it's written what it is one must do to kill back
in defense (or self-revenge).

My personality aint killed nobody.
Yet a cop pulls me over for a smokey exhaust
saying
        ''Hi, I'm your friendly noise
        abatement officer''
as he yanks me into Mission Station
for a 1968 traffic warrant
outstanding
despite the fact I didn't drive in 1968
I didn't know how!

Yet there it says on the Memory Bank
that I ''failed to heed direction signals''
& now I must not fail to heed bail money.

Department of Justice Saxbe says crime today
so high ''we'' maybe need a national police force
  A national police
  A natural police
  A naturally national
  A nationally natural

POLICE

Saxbe's personality is killing me.
The desk sergeant is killing me with his
bullshit stories about
his football hero son.
The draft nearly killed me
but a shrink wrote a note saying I had a ''brittle personality''
which didn't work half so well as my draft board
burning to the ground—

My personality's not gonna kill me
It's gonna reach out & become something else altogether
& if it kills anybody, I'll watch it as it disappears
into the flames of Reader's Digest
like a vine of a million
determined, smiling stars.

Mother Tube

''In keeping with Channel 40's policy
of bringing you the latest in blood & guts & in living color
you are going to see another first—
attempted suicide''

& with that bulletin 30-year-old
Chris Chubbuck put a gun to her head
& fatally obliterated herself
as her half-hour morning talk show
was being broadcast live by WXLT-TV.

Chris Chubbuck jumped the news,
                              the artist
participating in life
                    & not as objective
lackey of electrons scattering across her face
& falling into the laps of Executives
as coins.
            She scripted it
& acted her part, despondently her friends say,
but gratuitously & with wit the tube says.
She is now the sputtering death
of housewives, their mouths drooping,
froze in dawn postures of mop, of dish & of diaper
as she falls behind the news.

Even the newscaster a victim to ''technical difficulties''

Turn the channel & watch her resurrect.
3 test-tube babies announced to the world!
Poor Chris, it aint your fault.
The screen became so big
so as to embrace you like a cold mother.

Golden Oldie

for Alan Senauke

Nancy's out in Montana fighting forest-fires
in the Red Star All-Woman Firebrigade.

                                          I get
divorced & hug wife Pam in the marble hallway
where we felt irreconciliably different.

Alan decides Revolutionary Bluegrass music
will wrench him from SF & plant him into roots of Ithaca, NY.

A crackpot walks into our print shop
to demand stationery printed for the JOSEPH E. SPOTT
UNIVERSITY of which he is President Joseph E. Spott
& likewise head of a 90,000 member anti-rape organization
which shows as its logo a woman brutally raped
in switchblade style of S. Clay Wilson
& then he brusquely confides that he's the ''only Friend of Woman.''

Les & Kathie decide that they're a family
& decide the rigors of SF & Welfare & The Movement
drive them to spongey Shakespearean forests of Oregon
where they'll ooze in happy life & 2 kids.

Robin does piecework macramé flower-pot holders
& piecework counseling at Mt. St. Joseph's School for Delinquent Girl
(herself ex-delinquent girl).
She gets evicted from her home (with 11 Nash Metropolitans
junked in backyard)
for having a Farmworkers' poster up
which, in the eye of her landlord denotes
Headquarters for a Revolutionary Organization.

**Where is this revolutionary organization, anyway
that will twist this landlord's life?**

At this point, all I know is that I got divorced
& Alan leaves, yet my wife, now ex-, stays,
& I go on a honeymoon with Robin
to come back to find Alan going,
leaving me & the close friendship of years,
leaving our printing collective—

Quick, let's get a gold watch!

Let's get a gold poem, a solid goldie,
& presenting it I'll look in Alan's eyes steady & say:

"Take it easy, be strong.
This poem is a remembrance waking up
in the same room with you
like a flower doing jumping-jacks at dawn."

Uncle

All the women around me are having babies.
My ex-wife, ex-lovers, yet still-friends,
having babies & none of them "mine."
A friend I love now is having a baby
but neither is this by my doing & I
                              must learn to be Uncle.
I feel more & more out of it

until I realize the negative side of being "uncle"
has its positive side as well:

I think of Ho Chi Minh & why Vietnamese call him
Uncle & compare this Uncle to my own
to see if I could do so well or at least learn to be better than I am.

They call him Uncle Ho because, tho his
                              children are not his own
by birth he loves them just the same,
tho we would think he wouldn't love someone else's child
he does so nonetheless
& by choice
& by a love that goes beyond family
that, by careless reason, seems detached
& yet, for this very reason,

147

is precious even more,
more so because his love is proven by deeds
as well as poems
so that a young girl could put her head
on an old man's breast
& cry because her parents starve and suffer
& tears come to Uncle Ho's eyes
even with strong determination.

Uncle Ho, you are my uncle too
& I hope to learn from you,
to struggle, to love my children,
to act continually to win their love
by deeds
even in my small life
that is not Uncle to the peoples of the world
like yours.

ESCUELA DE LA REVOLUCION

Huelga at California Originals fabrica
where de-luxe pottery & dishery
grow from Mexicano hands
20 years & still $2.10 per hour

Huelga y unidad between
legal & ''illegal''
contra la Migra, los patrones y
Cabrones—
un daño contra uno es un daño contra
the vast working class deployed across
Los Angeles of petrochemical metalurgical
components of
       moola
          dinero
            y do-re-mi

pero **SOMOS TRABAJADORES
Y CREAMOS LA RIQUEZA**

& so **HUELGA**
despite golpes en la cabeza
in Los & San Pancho o Brooklyn
where *un daño contra uno*
becomes a flower
in the smudge

y la huelga becomes
a school for revolution
as huelgistas strain
at the centro cultural con
classic oil well humping in backyard
like a chicken pecking
at bones of padres

as la huelga becomes un acto,
workers learning teatro
to cantata from Chile,
Santa Maria de Iquique
as pottery workers
               Mexicano
become miners
             Chileno
porque un dano contra uno es

after rehearsal a serious
meeting to name themselves—
qué? quién?—
          la lucha de las
palabras es tambien
escuela de la revolucion
& they decide
after long debate

GRUPO DEL TEATRO POPULAR
                              DEL

MOVIMIENTO OBRERO

because this huelga
is more than one flicker
& the play these workers
move to is on a stage
as big as the vast
escuela de la revolucion

People of ethnic minority in Vietnam carry on their shoulders a house from their former concentration camp back to their home village after liberation.
Photograph from North Vietnamese News Service

MOVING DAY

Once again, instability wins out
& I gotta move.
The money siphons thru my fingers
from bank to landlord per usual
but now I gotta huff upstairs
hugging crates of momentos & hairbrushes & diapers.
After so many years, maybe this place I can stay put.
Maybe the roof won't leak or maybe I won't up & leave
& maybe no one'll get busted or divorced
& maybe sickness of decay of old society
won't clamp us shut like a vice-grip
in a mad scientist's nuclear masturbation fantasy.

Who knows?

I do know that many white folk
are not village-bound or single-placers.
We move around,
drawn by that same hoax
which drew packed boats of Polish peasants to imitation gold lamé
        streets of USA,
not like Vietnamese who now after liberation
pour back to ancestral homes
or like Oglala Sioux aiming their feet again to Wounded Knee

In my hollow living room I ponder:
The last Marine leaves Saigon
& as he gets yanked into the Chinook
helicopter in midst of Vietnamese tearing apart US embassy
a buddy grabs his arm & asks:
''What kinda Pizza you want
back at the base?''

It's moving day. / Vietnam has moved the world
& ''Pizza'' is the last word of US Death.
I laugh & join a chorus of joy.
Vietnam is home!
Welcome home, Vietnam!
I feel honored in my instability to have moved again at this time.
Despite all socks & underwear I scatter,
prospects have never been so good.

5

Intimacy Under Capitalism
Is Fantasy / Agony

Larry Felson

Falling In Love Again In A Bar In Portland

Watching the dark blue lights
flipping the girls into the mirrors,
the re-life there, light
consuming the taut and frightened bodies
of these dancers.
I see the blue light
forcing the flesh
into the mirror,
            receiving the dead eyes
      of the men in this bar.
Wondering how the eyes go dead,
who owns the light,
and how our bodies become blue flashing bodies
saying, ''Watch me, want me, I will give you
my mouth, I will touch you without entering,''
blobs of light sinking into the swollen anonymous
hearts, eyes, of these imperialist war heroes, or
            the light buried in the Vietnam jungles
of their wives
later that night;
or the next day, imagining
some other soft rape
at breaktime in the bathroom at work.
The girls stare at them, actually
thru them, one by one,
and the men, remembering themselves,
all thinking, ''It's me, she wants me,''
as the girls sit down in their eyes,
each man feeling, ''No one could touch you like I could.''
The mechanical killers in this bar
fantasizing a purity in the unknown flesh:
as if that were the only freedom.

Everyone surrenders to the lights in this bar,
and everyone knows
they keep us from what we are:
the war between faces, the lover who keeps leaving,
the radiance of suffering of the person we want to be,
making the body
            a cliff
                        to fall from.
They try to make
intimacy under capitalism
fantasy or agony.

A dancer, on the way to the stage,
brushes me,
her warm wet flesh on my arm.
The wilderness, then, in me,
the king killer, girl lover, music sucking,
woman worshipping love slave
flesh hunting in a bar in Portland.

The dancer,
turning into the blue flesh of my eyes
and smiling, understanding
more than I
her touch.
The lights suddenly stun me,
light burning into the bodies of strangers,
light wavering,
the flesh collapsing in an image of flesh,
everyone watching in the mirrors,
everyone so close in the shimmering
it is impossible to touch.
I feel a dull flashing going thru me, and out,
how soft I am,
how nice to be close to my softness,
not moved to this light,
this sensational blue flashing darkness
staying inside the flesh
making the heart die.

158

Getting up, seeing nothing,
a continual blurting of feeling,
the desire for real light.
I could love anyone.
Getting out of this place.
Everyone leaving together.

The Light on the Wall

Rain and the discovery of feeling.
A natural order.
A long rain
without interruptions of faces.
The small light in the room
withdraws to the corner
in parts, edges of feeling
dividing the flesh
into swords and mouths,
the light sucked into the corner,
blocking the windows,
destroying the closeness of trees.

The rain is pushing the light
at me, through me,
upsetting every balance,
looking for a way out.
The trees are waving at me
as if I were human,
the leaves clinging,
the branches reaching for the windows
in the slow rain.

This rain goes anywhere.
It is just light on the wall.
There are no swords or mouths
or beasts or Christs
or anyone calling to me.
What are we supposed to feel,
now, in this rain?
What kind of order
beside the movement of her mouth?
Should I watch the poor wet pigeons
take off and come down
on the aluminum roofs across the street?
Should I watch the streetfighting
and the studied genuflection after,
the sweet mouth's memory
suffering to be noticed?
I am aware of the light.
I am aware of the rain.
I am holding on to it.

The body is inspiration,
or separation from light.
Unnatural, passionate,
the body in hiding,
the body hiding
the missing part of the face.
''How long does love last?''
The thousand views of the natural,
the predicament of giving,
the possibility of forgetting everything.
Kill the natural order.
The rain will stop.
The light will become even.
Let the body go. Let the body go.

Birdblood

Hills and trees. Birds and bodies.
Your hand is near me.
Feels like I'm reaching thru a pool of leaves
into a river of bodies without faces.
There's nothing to know.
The flesh is the spirit.
The heart is a hatchet.
Trees are true.

There's
your hand.
Bacteria from the radioactive dinosaurs
patrolling our streets and bodies
fans out on my tongue.
I feel like a self butchering mule's head.
The blood from my eyes covers your body.
My love for you is a wavering twisting pain
going thru me like a fantasy of paradise.
My speech clots. The flesh hurts.
The flesh hurts to be known.
Caught in the crossflow of mouths, gunshots, and herons,
your hand, sweet dungmeat of desire
full of flowerblood, birdblood, flowerblood, birdblood,
flowerblub, birblub, flarbub, burblub, flurburb, blurburb,
flirblup, burplup, flurburb, burburblurb, flurblood,
burrrrbllluuuhhhh

Give me your hand.
The showering follicles of light
thrive on our
abandonment.
We have some contagious attraction
that will not redeem us
from our lips.
What light there is
seems to fall out of us
as desire.

In this instant,
as if some great injury in the universe
conspired against the heart,
we walk into the ocean

angels of moonlight, angels of flesh
who want to be loved forever.

The moon is drowning in your hair.
I love you forever.

The Face in the Body

Continuously apart from what I love,
trying to invent the feeling after,
watching an unknown body
crawl through the heap of lovers
disrobing again on the beautiful surface.

The beauty will hide me.
The body in the absence of need.
The dimness, the dimness of limbs,
trees or bodies,
the terrible distance, distance,
walking among leaves and hands
unable to feel anything.
The white morning light
and the blue morning light.

Sliding among the boneless faces,
killing ourselves in the glare from the flesh.
Where is the sense of closeness?
The body moves in its shadow,
destroying mouths, touching nothing
with its hot tongue,
succumbing to no one.

Your face is not failing.
Your face feels fresh,
floated with tongue and mouth,
body danced on,

kissed to the bone,
she-spirit underflow.

Will the kissing go down through the body,
challenging the still heart,
or stay on the tongue
as a stiffness at the center,
a decoy in the flesh,
kissing without touching?

I see your face in the body.
I feel the hand on my back entering,
as your mouth is leaving,
and I know the body feels
only the beginning of desire.

The further we go
the darker it gets.
White arms, white arms in the water
turning dark as they go down,
the pure white darkness in the flesh
getting darker as we go under.

Pulling the Heart Out

I put my hand inside the deer
and pulled out its heart.
It was very hard and tough.
It was the only part I wanted to keep.
But I put it in the bucket with the head and the intestines
and the lungs and the other organs and pieces of flesh
I tore out of the open rib cage.
I didn't want to know the names of the other organs,
or what they did, or why the blood flowed
from there to there.
I wanted to keep only the heart

but I threw it in the bucket.
I remember thinking it was hard and tough
like a steel breast or an excited tongue
at the instant of orgasm.

At night I wrote: "As if deer were not carnal. As if
the moon were just a light fixture hanging in the bathroom.
The light is eternal
until you turn the switch
off. I loved you like that. I love you like that.
Even now an immaculate jaundice of desire
haunts me."

Waking the next morning, a dream:
I'm falling behind holding a gun on the guards chasing us,
not firing when they charge,
feeling terror as they run over me,
as you run into the bucket of deer flesh.

When I touch you
I can't feel
the tone of your face.
No one turned the switch off
but the heart's in the bucket
anyway.

Drawing by Allana Lee

Notes from the Tenderloin

1

                  In your flesh
    an unknown privacy.
                          So far

     inside
the heart cannot imagine
      if this is what love is.
                          A sudden stillness
    striking thru the bloodstream
      making a wall of images
    we do not understand:
"The stinging music, the mountain of flesh,
  the snow water of the lake we're falling in."
These images, this writing,
                    as if entering your body
in need of tenderness and demons
and discovering the body
an obstacle to over come,
                  like the desire for death

2

                 My hands are on you.
     I feel them
closing on your wrist.   I lick your skin.
     I imagine your skin
        feels like it's being licked
    by the tongue of a monster,
a monster you love,
        the love (without desire)
    making you lonely,
      while I moan,

    a moaning we mistake for closeness.

3

                    Affected by her morning
flush.   I feel myself
not feeling it back.
I can't explain this negative
        force.   It's not
painful, but like pain
I believe it as absolute truth.   Her
touch bringing some awareness
            of what I can't feel.
She said: ''Your frantic uncontrollable affection—
but none of it for me.''
                    When I'm in her
    my body's in limbo, in hell, in love,
without the rest of me
                        I think ''I'm in my body
only when I'm in her body''

I glisten and suffer in her
afraid of her gentleness
imagining I love her

Her body does not believe what I imagine

4

I feel like a piece of electricity.
I is a piece of electricity.
My flesh generates this energy.
My span is the life of the sexual impulse
diluting into depth charges in the mind,
excavations by single beam light
among coral and fauna of emotion,
cracks in crevices in the brain
where the brain sprouts strange ruined flowers,
hybrid blossoms, erosions of stem and route,
tearducts pushing thru the head
into the energy, into the body,
musics, logics,
the disintegration we feel
each time we touch.

5

You touch me. I feel blank.
Blank war blank dying blank flesh blank
blood blank faces in misery lampshades walls
surfaces of light shadows indefinite objects instants of
self absence no one no world to belong to nothing undiscovered
but a slur of the mind into: confinement, resignation,
surface of pleasure, shame. Dust on the window.
Dust in the throat. No blood in the flesh.
No blood flowing thru the villages of Indochina,
no blood in Dallas, no blood at Attica or Soledad,
no blood in Birmingham or Detroit or Delano,
no death in Chile, no death in Greece,
no one dying in Brazil or Mozambique,
no blood in San Francisco,
no blood in the factories and bedrooms and freeways of Amerika,
only the frantic still skin
enfolding us in a closed universe
on the floor of my private room,
the flesh numb in a thinklessness,
feel-lessness, as if we're aware
only of sexual separate bodies
without any blood in them,
making the action of physically touching
impossible without pain or deception,
making the heart into a bottle of ten million birds,
a bottle of blood spilling anywhere,
the war in us anywhere, the war in the body,
the war in the street,
the war of avoiding each other:
in houses, in bed,
on buses, at the laundry, in movie lobbies,
cafes, bars, parking lots, urinals,
at work. Avoiding each other.

Walking thru SAFEWAY,
among the vegetables and tired strangers,
under fluorescent light

staring at the cauliflower
I see a vision of barbed wire meshed over heads,
the vision, shreds of a milky membrane
oozing thru metal fibres in the brain,
the heads stacked together burning and dying,
the fiery juice of their death
the mess in my heart I yield to, in this instant,
the vision, a magnetic sensation of the flesh
and its floundering sympathies.

Out of Safeway. The instant is over.
The people I see are stronger.
Our suffering is just a prelude
to our unity.
The great love we feel for each other
will destroy this mess, this capitalist mess,
and bring our lives together in a new world
of our own making.
The revolution will bring us together.

6

Wandering among the dying drunks and junkies
and ancient 19 year old girls of the tenderloin,
I see a filament of veins and hair in a passing face
and am drawn into this unknown person's possible pain,
as if there were an instantaneous natural bond of suffering
between us, as if I believed the obligation to respond
were a purity of spirit emptied in anyone's touch—
the right glance, somebody's hot hands, the deep kisses
from nowhere, the childhood pity, the sweet nightmare
of death in the falling thru his arms or her arms,
the imagined holiness of everyone but yourself,
everyone singing the sweet song of dead sweetness—
I want to say to you, I want to say to myself
this song obliterates our existence,
this sadness is a reflection of the dying
we believe we are caught in,
I want to say to you in your isolation and despair

that the famous beauty of individual private suffering
has no power over the oppressions of Amerikan capitalism
as it controls our daily lives,
that the internalized violence of emotions structured by
Amerikan capitalist culture determine our most intimate
moments, that the inability to see ourselves being
manipulated into self-torture by Amerikan capitalist society
makes us feel like worthless marginal hopelessly suffering
non-beings who exist in a dream of longing
where nothing will touch,
where we can't feel anything but pain.

And then shame.
For our lost selves.
It feels like unalterable incoherent isolation.

7

WE KNOW THE ENEMY: It is
the way our lives have been dominated
by capitalist modes of experience,
at work AND in love.
It is subservience to structures of reality
we were given as absolute truths
rather than what they are:
historical circumstances of capitalism.
It is the master-slave assumptions
underlying relationships between owner and worker,
parent and child,
lover and lover.
The enemy is the celebration of agony
manufactured, labeled, and distributed
under the laws of capitalist political economy.
Get the enemy—this complex set of strategies and structures
of capitalist domination—
out in the open
where we can see him and destroy him.

FIVE MUSK DEER, FRIGHTENED BY A PACK OF WILD DOGS
BAYING OUTSIDE THEIR ENCLAVE, JUMPED OVER A TEN
    FOOT FENCE
AND FELL DOWN AN EMBANKMENT ONTO THE FREEWAY
    BELOW
WHERE THEY WERE KILLED INSTANTLY IN THE
ONCOMING TRAFFIC

We want no song but the body against death song
as our love for each other takes power
over our lakes and skies and cities and bodies,
as our love takes power over our own bloodstream.

A Wave of Submission

(Vancouver-to-Portland)

A wave of submission
                            in the tunnel.
        Into the slits.
                    Powerful blankness
of light,
            light taking me out
        to a feeling of nearness,
a nearness for them that, who are
            in me, the them
        getting further away
in our histories, but closer,
closer,
            in giving a place to respond to.
                My Aunt Fanny, 92,
excited reliving the difference between
''getting married under the sky,''
the way she did, on the
                Winepah farm in Saskatchewan in 1898,
                    (The difference—
and what it means now.

I think, ''What is our sky?''
        The equivalents or REORDERINGS
of farm and sky.   Thinking
of the inability to be concrete, to understand
what I feel—why it's so hard to accept
the facts of my existence
            when they aren't images of anything else,
the difficulty of writing this
as I break into the lyrical chain, though real,
I was trying to follow   driving toward Portland.
The farm and the sky.
Our street has
no sky. The heart's in
struggle. The heart is against
imperialism. Intimate and political.
The re-ordering is getting the heart to need
socialism and revolution
as much as it wants
erotic one-to-one affection.
            Encountering my family
makes me want to ask—I'm going 75 miles-an-hour,
farms on both sides,
under a wood smoke sky
why do I need an image for the color of the sky?
Why a meaning for this light?)
ask, what should live?

San Diego

I connect with your body
as if we were blossoms
floating on a volcanic lake
where every touch
is a plunge into molten lava.

I am paralyzed by your wet loins.

What I feel is, ''Leave me alone, loins.''
My tongue is like tin foil in your teeth
and I love you.
I pretend to exist
by disrupting any emotion
that pleases.
The only thing real, besides your mouth,
is what feels like
it has never been felt before.
I try to feel this instant
eternally. But nothing is still
invisible
and we are afraid of it.
Love becomes breaking the law,
light and affection become torments of the imagination,
the heart gets tricked by longing
into a salvation of dark forests of impersonal tenderness,
this or that sudden final choice,
waterfalls of foreign sweat,
lips of stone flesh
bringing an avalanche of starshit, of desire,
        love being as vague and consuming
as the romantic poetry this poem tries to deny
but gets lost in, as the silly images
poets and lovers use
to con themselves out of the actual circumstances
of their lives. Images like
sparrows whose wings are made of concrete
buried in pigeon shit. I already said dark forests
and tin foil and blossoms and volcanic lake and shoreline
and stone flesh and waterfalls and leave me alone, loins.
Have your loins become images to be read in a poem
that is not a poem
but only a tone in my voice?

The circumstance of this poem is:
I am in San Diego. It's 2:15 AM. I'm
sitting in my car in an alley

behind a bar.
People are going home with strangers.
They're talking about
"partying."
"Don't move,"
I feel.

How do you do
THAT? Act
like a piece of
machinery,
or drunk
or dead
DON'T
COMPLETE
this thought.
I imagined I
was going to be killed
by an unknown woman in this alley.
That this moment
without you
is final.
That love is final and I don't know HOW to love
or when it IS love—my body won't tell me—
and my body is in a death-like trance of passion
looking at an unknown woman

Greyhound Meditation: The Santa Ana Freeway

Locked in the toilet, reading the Los Angeles Times:
economy getting worse, unemployment and prices rising,
cops shoot kid in back—a Black kid from Compton—
"running from a joyride in a stolen car."
My eyes slip to the Coppertone ad
of the bare-assed little girl with a sunburn.

Getting excited and hating it,
I drop the paper, look up at the graffiti on the walls,
take out a pen and begin writing, at 30 years old, my first graffiti:
''Nothing is as natural as the ability to resist—''
a quote from George Jackson.
Looking at it I feel suddenly beautiful,
my tongue touching the sweet saliva on the roof of my mouth,
feeling calm and sweaty, feeling safe inside this action,
getting high from it—when someone knocks to get in.
I am instantly panicked and angry
as if caught in a dream with my pants down
by the police or my mother and rush to get out.
I get up, button my pants, turn the water on loud in the sink
as a decoy for more time, pick up the newspaper
and jam it into the wastebasket,
reach for the door to go out,
remember I have to turn the water in the sink OFF,
reach back and twist the handle violently,
see the toilet,
grit my teeth in a rage
realizing I haven't flushed it yet,
flush it,
and for one endless instant
see myself in the mirror trying to appear calm and detached
like a ''normal'' person coming out of the bathroom
on the Greyhound bus on the Santa Ana Freeway
between Los Angeles and San Diego in the summertime.

I open the door and go out.
An old woman, smiling, goes in.
Back in my seat, watching everyone close to me:
two bored Black kids in levi jackets,
an old white guy who looks like a retired Navy chief
drinking wine from a paper sack,
a thin Chicano woman with short hair
chewing gum. Everyone staring at something.
I think, AT WHAT KEEPS US APART. Apart from what?
I take my notebook out of my bag and write: ''APART FROM
    WHAT?''

Looking out the window, trying to find some way
to care about what's out there.
I begin writing what I see:
Power lines, SHELL E-Z-ON ENTRANCE, a new lane of traffic,
MONTEBELLO NEXT EXIT, 76 E-Z-RETURN, unfinished wall,
exit lane, concrete and dirt, some trees on an embankment,
a call box, one tree on the edge of a flat empty parking lot
with lights, an arrow, GREAT WESTERN SHOWGROUNDS,
an empty parking lot with lights, a huge marquee
shaped like a cartoon cowboy holding a cloud with the caption:
SUPPORT MARCH OF DIMES, wooden fence piled up,
a modern flat school, rough grass field, B.F. GOODRICH,
JIM BEAM, gigantic Egyptian frescoes on a monolithic building,
backyards of houses and trees, TV antennas,
a block long red and white warehouse next to power towers,
in the background snow on the mountains,
the sky red and molten, 1ST WESTERN BANK building, RCA
    building,
WELLS FARGO, KENT, huge 1ST WESTERN sign hanging
almost over the freeway, power lines, thirty-nine power towers
counted into the distance, a highway under construction
beneath us, telephone poles, wires, MAJESTIC REALTY,
FIRESTONE, gigantic three-sectioned smoking factory complex
with no signs on it, LEVER BROTHERS building made of
what seems like massive rolls of aluminum tubing, VICEROY
billboard, GERMAIN MOORE MACHINERY CO. neon sign,
OLYMPIA IT'S THE WATER, OLD CROW, STANDARD,
ZIEGLER STEEL SERVICE CORPORATION (a block square),
YOKOHAMA TIRES, ENCO, MEDIN HEALTH SUPPLY,
HALO LIGHTING DIVISION, McGRAW-EDISON,
STATE DIVISION OF HIGHWAYS, TEXLITE, HALORAN
    HARDWARE,
a valley of new houses, ARCO, STANDARD OIL, a football
    stadium,
ground being dug for a track field, CAL STRIPPING COMPANY,
MONTEBELLO EXIT.
Montebello exit. We're stalled in traffic.
We've been travelling for two miles on this bus

and at 60 miles-an-hour that's about two minutes.
Two minutes and two miles,
and I've recorded only a small part
of what I've seen.
We start moving. The anger continues to rise.
It's hard to look directly for even two minutes
at what's been done to our lives
by those big companies and the pimps and whores
of advertizing out there along the freeway.
OUT THERE? That's OUR
LIVES. What's happening outside the bloodstream
is happening inside.
It makes me scared of my own
authenticity.
I see a pair of hands going by in a passing car window,
clasped, rocking up and down, and for a second
I feel the energy of affection overtake me
as it did in the bathroom, and I wonder whether
the girl in the Coppertone ad was ever someone real,
and whether I'm ever real and whose fault this is
and what this has to do with
the almost ecstasy of hatred I feel
looking out the window at the Southern California
freeway landscape.

NOTHING IS AS NATURAL AS THE ABILITY TO RESIST

San Francisco 1975

1

Working in a warehouse
of broken necks
of long chained lamps
            perfumed with
plywood and silver black

dust—   Standing
amid condemned scales, cardboard baskets, and metal bowls
of trash,
working under a huge roof of broken windows
compressing the sky into small fibres of grey light
that crack on the floor over chalk scrawls of faces
and fences and concrete moons,
over smears of grease in the shadows
beneath monumentally awkward tilting pillars
that stagger in the floating dust,
sections and strands and folds of strange abrupt light
focusing my eyes on the faces of the others
working in this warehouse of shattered industrial light,
lying on our backs in the cold asphalt dust
fixing corroded broken-down voting machines,
loading and unloading 1200 pound 60 year-old metal monstrosities,
warming to the glances and movements and labor
of other workers,
looking up to the same rain on the cracked windows,
Luis and I notice some words painted over a ''No Talking'' sign;
the words say:
        THE PEOPLE UNITED WILL NEVER BE DEFEATED—
        THE REVOLUTION LIVES!
And we believe it
because
we can see it
all around us
in our   eyes.

The city in burning blue fog.
Walked her home. Frail night. Walls of moonlight.
Engines and voices and moaning.
Slurred and troubled speech.
Talk of relationships of other people.
She looking at me—
I notice the stars

do not exist
except when we imagine
nothing real
but ourselves.
No kiss.

After, walking down the Leavenworth street hill,
feeling, ''starlust'', ''melancholy'', ''bliss'',
pulled by the fiery damp darkness,
by faces in windows,
by night flowers and far-off sudden longing,
by the lights quivering and bleeding in the bay,
entering a stream of energy
felt as liquid expansions and barriers of love and denial
emerging spread out in language
as a blasted and blasting furnace of self-isolating desire,
the skin of my beloved beloved beloved
unravelling in the sheets
without any direction, without feeling
where we are, but feeling
fierce intimate soft groping movements
fusing in the flesh
into visions of slow falling saffron limbs—our own
transparent and glowing from within,
immense and blazing movements
of legs, arms, heads,
red and silver armors of flesh, moaning limbs,
whole torsos churning in air, in actual bright light,
this light from the movement of limbs
I trust like a piece of starlight
swallowed by the brain,
splitting into the universe
or paradise your tongue protects—
a flesh that exists beyond touching.

Shall the intoxication of skin
have no other consequence
but feathers of flesh

washing thru us
slowly corroding any other sense?
There's light on the fringes of buildings.

3

From the air
I see white morning light
over the bay
and nothing is unreal,
all is extensions of, completions of
moving in your body.
Looking thru clouds,
looking thru sunlight and water,
I feel a sudden horror of
the music of the body
and no other freedom.
A self-extinction
by flesh.
Looking thru air.

White foam. Wings of flesh
glide by like lips. Images,
they are not flesh. They're not even
lips.
They are fragments of clouds
but they break thru the traditional
dead boundaries imposed by language and the life and death
we feel approaching in who we love. We demand or deny
the service of who we love. I see wet canyons
coiled under dry ridges. I see grids of rocks
and labyrinths of mountains and trees and this is all literally
seen and it results in a non-literal unseen waft of the presence of
wings of rapture, I have to call it, that occurs
BECAUSE of the absence of history,
of the absence of myself in history
or as history.
The RAPTURE on this plane looking down on the Southern
    California

coast suddenly
turning into a desire
to know the suffering
of the people of Hiroshima and Nagasaki,
recalling the rapture of the atomic physicists
who, it was reported, ''rushed to order champagne dinners
when the news came the thing had worked.''

The thing had worked.
I think I see Einstein
climbing thru the maze of lights
blinking on and off in the huge power station below
as we fly over San Pedro.
I see the shadow of 8 million people
crossing the flat moving skin of Los Angeles
all calling to each other.
Actually I see a lot of wires and billboards
and cars and colors and trees and buildings
and that's about all.
How to advance our lives out of the ideological and
material consumer-spectator existence we pretend to ignore
or avoid. We make up images to survive,
evading the actual conditions of our lives.
Making the body
into a burning boat,
moaning about the heat,
and not caring about the source of the flames.
What is the capital of the bloodstream?
Capitalism determines even our most intimate moments.
The social order is also an internal order.
When you begin to lose your capitalist structure
you begin to feel the end of one form of desire
and the beginning of another.

Aren't you my love with wings of RAPTURE? (the INSIDE calling)
Where are you?
I am ready to forgive (to recognize?) your absence.
Soon to arrive in the chains of sweetness.

I was told the body was the entrance. The chaos of certainty.
A mouth I could trust.

In self-anger,
in dreaming of your
one touch, dreading
desire,
dreaming of waking in
mouth branch flow
of eye rain
in dim throat
morning wandering
flesh sound sung
and then
the plane crash
into your actual lips.

4

Our lips contact memories of deadness
The deadness feels like lillies writhing
In furnaces of burning mouths
The heart is a handgun of business proposals and anonymous lust
Kisses are losses
The body is baby blue shit of capitalist intimacy
The fleshspirit is made-up by the State   We are
Churned into Skippy peanut butter and blue chip stamps
Stuck on anybody
Our language is private, like private investment bank accounts,
Stocks, collaterals, dividends, options—the language itself
Engulfs us—blue chips, blue shit, market values up and down,
Surplus value, distant rainfall, distant rainfall
All this abstract stuff
the devils and angels of capitalism we are taught to believe in
As truth
Taught to deceive ourselves, as if
The heart had no history, as if the heart were
A piece of milk blown up by mother,
Atomic milk we search for in the arms of others

5

On the 5PM freeway to Sacramento
the Standard Oil refinery in the hills
spurts out purple smoke over the water,
the cows in the dark fields eat smoky grass,
we drink smoky milk,
and the milk company owners wallow in the milky green slime
churned from their workers' blood.

The cows seem almost beautiful in the purple smoke,
the same burning purple
I imagine rising from the villages of Southeast Asia,
thin purple smoke of American Imperialism
so unnatural and deathlike
it compels us to destroy its source.

The source: capitalism, exploitation, profit, the ruling class,
division of labor, racial oppression, the oppression of national
minorities, the oppression of women, sexual oppression, the
        oppression of old people
and young people, the oppression of all workers, capitalism.

Not very pretty sounding. Not poetry. No images to relieve you
or rob you from your anger.

No matter.
The people who made this road, who make these cars,
and who work these fields
are rising up

to take back what belongs to us—
cows, milk, fields, oil, freeway, flesh—our own lives.

6

This older Russian lady with red hair
wearing a worn-out but immaculate black coat
kept repeating to the butcher at Safeway,

loudly, in a thick Slavic accent,
that she wanted something special.
But nobody, especially the butcher,
could make out what she was saying.
She was patient, very patient,
saying it slower and louder each time,
the butcher getting more and more impatient,
half-annoyed, half-in-sympathy.
Pretty soon a small crowd gathered,
everyone calling out words and phrases
trying to figure our what she wanted:
Skewered prawns? Stewed buns? Should have phoned?
Sutured bone? Sure the bomb? Super bowl?
Checkered fawn? Sugar buns? Suck her plums?
Sewer born? Stew your own?
Azure palm?

A guy behind me finally calls out, ''Hey man, she want SUGAR BONE,
you know, for the dog.'' Everyone started laughing.
But she said, not laughing, slowly and loudly
in her thick accent, ''Yes, that is right, SUGARBONE. For soup.''
The butcher, troubled, said, ''Oh yeah, sugarbone.
I think we got some in the back.''
He went to get it
while she waited, it seemed,
defiantly,
and we went away
all
not laughing.

7

Dancing under the skin of animals,
dancing the ripe death of flesh,
her mouth is a little closer.
Like a sliced and bloody angel
turning human in the struggle.
I hear the bottom of her heart.
It's a streetfight started by a final kiss,

a momentary screech of lips on calm skin.
Blood moves thru blood
to bone.
The heart is bone.
The heart is a trap.
If you gnaw it,
it turns to sugar
and will eventually
rot your system.
The flesh is now
a dangerous myth.
Like birdsong
or morning light.
Like, ''The ocean is ending,''
or, ''Desire is an unknown enemy
living in your touch.''

I can't see what I feel. The sweetness doesn't die.
The fog is exactly
touchless. In it naturally
move all people, their machines, and their
dead or blooming gardens.
The gates are made of flesh
and feel like flesh
but are much deeper.
They are made of guns, history, and lies.
We will break them with guns, history, and truth.
We're beyond what's only
self.
FEEL   OUR   NEW   FLESH

Authors' Notes

Hilton Obenzinger
by Steve Brooks

Beau Beausoleil
by Denis Koran

Stephen Vincent
by Wilfred Q. Castaño

Steve Brooks
by Hilton Obenzinger

BEAU BEAUSOLEIL

For six years I wrote poetry from my wrist down and used up a lot of energy in an effort to stay dead. Laura finally forced my "hand" by breaking open both our marriage and our lives. I moved to the Tenderloin and with my defenses down poetry rushed up my arms into my life. These poems are the beginning of an effort to locate my roots, my speech, my participation with you.

STEVE BROOKS

I was talking about my obsessions. The man said, "It sounds like you're obsessed with your obsessions." During the time this collection was in process I had stopped writing. I was performing on stage. Now I'm painting again after 12 years. In response to Diane Dunn's indignant disbelief at Bill & Leslie's wedding in '64, "I cannot play the guitar." An abiding urge to produce continues. The forms change. If you judge that I suffer from this disparation, that's OK. Male Liberation will yet release us both from such a concern. As my son said recently, "Everything about a banana is appealing."

The poems of mine in this anthology represent the period 1970-1975, when I was going thru a transition from isolated elitist ''poet,'' half heartedly digging in the rotting graveyard of the petty-bourgeois literary world, to making contact with the vaguely ''anti-Imperialist'' petty-bourgeois social reformist coalitions, liberal movements for ''equal rights under capitalism,'' and various bourgeois nationalist groups consciously or unconsciously aligning themselves with the policies and practices of the revisionist CP-USA.

Since that time I've seen that petty-bourgeois leftists—whether extremists, reformists, or grass-roots populists—are almost always cut off from the masses of working people, are out for their own individual opportunist goals, and end up selling out the working class and other oppressed people. Over the past few years, I've come to take the fighting stand of the working class, and have begun to learn how to help build a mass movement capable of overthrowing capitalist rule. These poems are a record of my own particular struggles against the petty-bourgeois life and ideas I was born into, and the beginning consciousness—both personal and historical—that capitalist society is rotten and dying and that the only solution for the masses of people is revolution led by the working class and the establishment of socialism. In order to write from this stand, the class stand of the revolutionary proletariat, writers from the petty-bourgeois have to undergo what Mao calls, ''a change of feelings, from one class to another.'' Mao goes on: ''If our writers and artists who come from the intelligentsia want their works to be well received by the masses, they must change and remould their thinking and their feelings.'' To do that writers must change their actual lives and enter the revolutionary struggle on the side of the working class to end the system of wage slavery and exploitation, to end the blood-sucking rule of capitalism ONCE AND FOR ALL.

The future is gonna be great. The older I get the more whole I feel. The older I get the more US imperialism spirals into the pits. What a great time to live! Now, youth is splendid, although adolescence has a tendency to be hell. Getting to be old has its hollow moments too. Living here in San Francisco gets clearer as time does the bump. Actually the future might be temporarily dismal—particularly for revolutionaries. The rich have a tendency towards murder. But, in the end, what's inevitable will be very sweet. I'm looking forward to the future.

So far as the past is concerned. Well, I zigzagged through the US growing up. Early I became an activist, stormed around in the civil rights movement, the anti-war movement, went to Columbia University, engaged in 1968 student strike. I lived up North about 300 miles on Hoopa Indian reservation, came down here to join up with whatever would move things forward, now work in FITS Printing collective and the SF Printing Coop which is an amalgam of many groups. I used to write poems a lot more than I do now. Trouble was I didn't say anything particularly important or true. In fact I used to think that great art was a great lie. Many writers think this. These people get grants and all that. Sort of like hanging a curtain across a canyon, that kind of stuff. The government likes paying people to say nothing. Anyway, I broke away from that and now I write only when it's just right. I don't consider myself a poet. I'm a talker on paper. Actually I print the shit all day—paper that is—and one gets a mundane attitude towards literature. More than anything I'd like a socialist revolution. That's the most mundane thing around—real practical—and out of that will come really exhilarating poetry.

I'm glad you were able to read these poems. To me they show how one person changes. I'd like to know what you think of them, what kind of poems or talk you do. Write to me in care of Momo's Press and I'll try to answer. I think it's that simple.

STEPHEN VINCENT

As I write this I am flying at 30,000 feet from New York to San Francisco. I am 35 years old. I have written, as they say, three books and numerous articles. If I fell out of this plane, that is slightly ruffled at this bouncy point, the air would not care what I have done, but drop me back to the ground where (God, we're over Pittsburgh) I would have to get back to San Francisco where I live with Debra McGee and two cats, Esther and Kuchar. And though Debra tells me yesterday morning on the phone that the four story Victorian flat right next door was almost burned to the ground, I continue to perceive a life full of possibility that is both personal and political, full of acts of feeling and strength. And God, perish my radical thoughts, even families of sorts. But as is, as this life goes, when I am not lazy or frightened, I stay alert to the inside and out to make beauty of the work, the pain and the love.